JOAN: DROP DEAD DIVA

JOAN: DROP DEAD DIVA
Rafal Kudlinski

2015

Copyright © 2015 by Rafal Kudlinski.
All rights reserved.
ISBN: 978-83-931465-0-5

Title: Joan: Drop Dead Diva (First Edition Feb. 2015)
Country of first publication: Poland
Published by: ITQ Media Publishing House
Cover art by: Piotr Mieczkowski and Rafal Kudlinski

No part of this publication may be reproduced, distributed, or transmitted in any form or by any means, including photocopying, recording, or other electronic or mechanical methods, without the prior written permission of the author, except in the case of brief quotations embodied in critical reviews and certain other non-commercial uses permitted by copyright law. This book is a satire and total work of fiction. Some names and identifying details have been changed to protect the privacy of the people involved

For more information about the author visit the website at: http://www.rafalkudlinski.com

Special Thanks and Acknowledgements

- Many thanks to Joan Rivers for thousands of hours of fun. Whether it was on TV or in the books, you were an inspiration for this novel. I sincerely hope you are having even more fun, wherever you are. You will be greatly missed!
- Many thanks to my best friend Piotr Mieczkowski for assembling such a great cover for the book. You always deliver exceptional results. Thanks Bro!
- Katarzyna and Monika, I do not know if I deserve such fantastic friends/fans. I love you babes.
- Big thanks to people who donated through crowdfunding campaign: Piotr Sokołowski, Chris Thornborrow, Bartosz Londzin, Krzysztof Minicki, Paweł Matysiak. You ROCK!

To my Mom and Grandmother.
Thank you for being coolest, fun and caring,
loving and plain awesome!
Love Ya!

About the Author

Rafal Kudlinski is a Polish physicist and journalist. His career choices were very diverse. During high school years, he was fascinated by science-fiction television shows like *Quantum Leap, Buck Rogers in the 25th Century, Alien Nation* and *Time Trax*, which led him to the first stage of his education as a physicist. In 2003, he graduated from Wroclaw University of Technology with a degree in computer physics. During his studies, he became obsessed with Hollywood stars. When Internet approached "BigBang" years, he started to create websites for all the stars he loved and admired, starting with Scott Bakula and ending with Hugh Jackman. He was an avid viewer of E! Entertainment network and always dreamed to work for this crazy channel. Unfortunately, life took a different turn and led him once again in a different direction to pursue a stable career. In 2004, he graduated from Wroclaw University of Economics with post-grad diploma in quality assurance. Life was good and he had a steady job, but the dream of becoming a journalist and the desire to become a part of the media world started to bite again. In 2008, he started his third degree in Journalism and Social Communication at the University of Wroclaw, and graduated in 2010. The same year he started NEWSFix Magazine with his best friend Piotr and also published his first book on themed television channels, which he dedicated to students of journalism. *Joan: Drop Dead Diva* is his first novel, which he decided to write the moment he heard Joan Rivers is dead. Joan was very special to him. As much he admires true artists he hates pseudo-celebrities who have nothing special but gain popularity with the masses.

Dear Reader/Friend!

First of all, a big THANK YOU for purchasing this book. I sincerely hope you enjoy reading it as much as I enjoyed creating it. The reason for writing this "fantasy" adventure was simple. We have lost one of the best comediennes that graced our planet so far. Joan Rivers was unique, at times harsh and bitchy, but in most cases very accurate with her jokes. *Joan Drop Dead Diva* is the first part in trilogy that will be published during the next few years.

To enjoy this book even more, please turn on and listen to your favorite music. It can be catchy pop songs or classical music, whatever tricks your body to feel good.

All the best!
Rafal

Come on ... Turn the music on ...:)
Believe me, reading experience will be more enjoyable.

CHAPTER ONE
Departure and Arrival

Where the fuck am I? Shit, my voice is back and I sound better than Britney during her last Las Vegas concert. It's strangely quiet here.

Mhmm… It must be it then… I kicked the bucket… I am Drop Dead Diva now….

I wondered what will happen next and guess what, I saw the door with "Exit" sign. I thought, that looks bad. Son of a bitch will have me now. But I am, shit, was a comedienne I never meant to hurt anyone. OK I stood up and approached the door with slight uncertainty. It would be stupid of me to knock but actually I did. No response… Went for the handle and pressed it. The door opened and there was a fucking bright light.

Great, I have problems with my voice and you want me to be freaking blind too? Unknown power sucked me into the brightness. I felt a little dizzy. After awhile I saw a red carpet and there was a huge roar coming in my direction... Marilyn? Audrey? Cary? ... I didn't know whether it was because of this bright light or I was hallucinating. I rubbed my eyes and looked again... I am in heaven, I thought, when everything suddenly paused and I heard a voice.

- Dear Joan it's not heaven yet. Where you will go for the eternity depends on your behavior. You have three earth years to prove, if you deserve eternal star treatment. Here is your guide. Meet Anne Frank. She will help you settle down in your new home in Hollywood-end. OK, I am messing with you now Joan. It's somebody very sweet and nice. Nevertheless beware and try to be kind.

OMFG! for the second I was shocked. Anne Frank. I thought I would finally meet this fabulous writer of the 20th century. But hey joke is on me now.

I like it here. You have great sense of humor God. It's gonna be a fun ride. Let's meet my assistant.

- Oh hello? Anybody there? Aaaaaaaahhhhhh ...

I opened my left eye and noticed I was in bed. Was it just a dream? Everything seemed in place, nothing was moved.

- Hello Joan. How are you ... It's me Anne Frank.

Noooooooooo...

* * *

- I am just messing with you. My name is Mary, Mary Fischer. You must be exhausted after... you know what.

I looked at that naughty Mary with "The Look" and answered

- Mary, Mary, Mary ... You too? Come on babe let this Anne Frank rest in peace. It's not funny anymore.

I looked around and it seemed I know the place but was not quite sure. The bed I was sitting on was exactly the same I had in New York, but the room was kind of different. It had two huge windows, a sofa and two armchairs with a beautiful little wooden table in between. Room was in immaculate condition. I turned my head to the right and noticed a fireplace. Just above it there was a lovely painting of a castle near the lake. I approached it and read down below. What? Prince Charles? OK, now I have seen everything.

Fireplace housing was made of fabulously designed marble with a curious looking switch on top of it. You know me I always have to check everything, so I pushed it. Suddenly a picture that was hanging above started to turn around and in a matter of seconds changed to a widescreen television set. It turned on automatically and I noticed a familiar logo on the screen.

It was not E! I worked for all these years. It was Celebrity Network, another trashy channel with fucked up pseudo-celebs wanting attention, I thought. I loved my job of bringing down these idiots without talent. I let it play and went for the door as I heard someone wanted eagerly to get into my room. I didn't knock this time, hahaha.... I pressed the handle and saw my precious Max looking at me. You son of a bitch (at least in that case I did not offend anyone now). My eyes got wet and I started to cry. I missed my dear friend so much. It was so hard to let him go last year. But hopefully now we will spend eternity together.

I started to go by the corridor in search of bathroom and wardrobe.

-Oh Joan, you have to be ready in 30 minutes. We have a meeting scheduled.
-30 minutes? Are you kidding me? I would need some black magic to get me ready in a such a short period of time. Unless you want me to scare hell out of them, I am ready now babe.
-What is the meeting about anyways?
-I'll describe everything in the limo. Now please get ready as we can't be late.

I rushed to the bathroom, got myself fixed as quickly as possible and made not scary enough for people to see me. Not really me, but hey I do not want to spend eternity listening to Rhianna without playback or babysitting Justin Bieber type of brat.

CHAPTER TWO
What the f**k is this place?

The house I was staying at was very nice. Not my type but at least furniture was the kind I would buy for myself. The wardrobe was big enough and had many beautiful evening dresses and outfits that are more official. I always wanted to look fabulous; maybe that's why I went bezerk with all these cosmetic enhancements. That's not the point now. I put on a dress that looked more official for the meeting as I had no freaking idea what was it about and went downstairs in search for Mary.

Mary was a very beautiful young woman in her 30s. She had long brown hair and green eyes. She had a spark in her eyes just like Audrey Hepburn at that age. It was very hard to turn away and stop looking at her. She seemed so genuine, authentic and totally not artificial. Dressed in light summer colors was a pure joy to the eye. She must be my guardian angel or something.

* * *

I noticed Mary sitting on the terrace and drinking coffee from an exceptionally crafted transparent cup. She turned around and looked at me with a smile.

- Oh Joan. You look very pretty. Please, have a cup of coffee and sit with me. We still have 15 minutes left.

For the moment I thought. Was she kidding? It took me at least 2 hours to make myself useful. What kind of time do they have in here? Doesn't matter as long as she's happy.

- Thank you Mary. Could you please tell me more about what am I doing here? What is this place? Is this my type of heaven, hell or something in between?

Mary looked directly into my eyes and said,

- Joan, this is neither heaven nor hell. You have been very good at what you had done in your first life. As we have to live in Hollywood-end for eternity, we need your help to clean up once to be unbelievable area full of artists with dreams and hopes for wonderful eternity. Right now Hollywood-end lost its magic and we think you can bring back the style, grace and talent to our community.

Well, well, that's good news. The worst that could happen would be to have empty calendar and nothing to do for eternity.

- Do you have any plans for this Mary?

- Actually, Yes I do. It's time to go now. I'll tell you more in the limo.

We finished our coffees and went through the hall to the front door. During the walk I noticed many familiar photos but couldn't remember who the people on them were. Is my memory failing? One picture was bound in Faberge frame and there was a collection of beautifully crafted eggs nearby. When we left outside, limousine was already waiting. Nothing fancy, but a simple new black Lincoln Town Car. Finally, I could see where I am. This is really it, Hollywood-end sign on the hill. If this world is an exact copy of Hollywood, I think I am nearby Lake Hollywood Park. But I have to ask Mary what kind of stuff she prepared for me.

I got into the car. Mary sat in front of me, smiled and opened her calendar.

- OK Joan. Here's how it goes. We have 3 years to straighten things up. People do not know who you are. You may recognize many of them, but they are not who you think they are. They may seem familiar to what you remember from the past, but this will change in a time.

- So does this mean I will lose all my memories of people I loved?
- Exactly. You have to leave everything behind and focus on what is here and now.

That sucks, I thought. But what the f**k can I

complain about. I am dead! So the only thing is to go with the plan and clean this shithole.

- As you have probably already started to notice, all your aches and health problems are disappearing. You won't be an 81-year-old lady anymore. For others you will look like a fabulous, eloquent lady in her 40s. You will have your own talk show on Public Television Station related to what is happening in Hollywood-end. You know the drill. You already had that kind of assignments in the past.

CHAPTER THREE
I am job, I am job

We have been driving for some time now. It's hard to keep track on time here as everything seems to be very slow. I looked through the window and noticed we have been driving on N Highland Ave. Sun was starting to rise and sky was beautifully blue with few clouds, almost like in the intro of "The Simpsons". Kids were in the queue waiting to enter the school. Kids here, I thought.

- Mary are these kids dead too?
- Yes they are. But at least here they can live and enjoy whatever they have missed in the first life.

I briefly smiled and thought about my grandson. I miss him so much.

As we've been driving, I have focused on one particular billboard with an ugly bimbo. Who the fuck is that? Big tits, fat ass, face like a used vagina. There was a note "Watch Meet the Farthashians" on Celebrity Network every night.

- Mary who are these Farthashians?

- Oh my Lord, where to start. This family is unbelievable. They came out of nowhere but people who live here love them as they were someone special. This is one of the cases you will work on, but not now. You will have plenty of time to get rid of them from public life.

Driver slowed down a bit. I opened the window and looked at the people as we passed by them. Some of them were happy, some sad. There were homeless people lying on the sidewalk. Are you fucking kidding me? Is this the road to heaven? Can these people have a break after death? Anyone pinch me. This is real not to be Holly "fucking" wood I know.

Mary looked at me and said,

- We're almost there. Public Television Station is the biggest and best television channel in Hollywood-end. We have the best people working for us. Even though we're the biggest, Celebrity Network is gaining better results every month with its trashy programs and its stars. People are watching "Meet the Farthashians", "Cleaning Ladies of Hollywood-end", "Divas without the Voices", "Housewives from the Sexy Mansion" or the latest "Spoiled and Dumb Kids of Beverly Halls". As you can see it's hard to call it quality viewing. We need old Hollywood-end and you are here to help us get it back.

- It looks like our Hollywood. Dumb celebs and nothing to laugh about.

Having said that, we arrived at the studio. And it was huge. The entire building was made of glass in the shape of a TV. It was kind of funny looking one. From the distance you could distinguish all the features of an old looking TV set from the 1980s. I wonder if there is another one that looks like VCR. Holly mother of Jesus, there is one. As we passed by the main building and went for the back entrance, there were two more buildings, one looked like VCR and the other like an old computer. I wonder if Steve Jobs works there, hahaha....

We stopped near the entrance. It was simply amazing. Several shaped fields of beauteous flowers and gorgeous looking palm trees between them. Smell was unbelievable.

We entered the building. Two nice looking guys were sitting at the reception. They stood up when we passed by them. I said, "Good Morning", and gave them a big smile. I am starting to like being 40-something years old bombshell again. I even winked at them. What the hell, I still got it ;). We approached and entered the elevator. Mary pushed 7th floor.

※ ※ ※

The ride was quick and we arrived to the destination in no time. My assistant was already waiting in front of the elevator door.

- Good Morning.

I have replied with the same.

- Hello, How do you do?
Mary started the formal introduction and said.

-Joan, this is Monique Szymolinsky, she will be your personal assistant. Monique, this is Joan, new daytime talk show host.

For a second I thought, another fucking foreigner. Linsky, Linsky ..., shit, she could almost be my family.

- Hi Mon, what's up?
- I am job, I am job ...

What the hell is this? Does that bitch speak any English? Or is this Mrs. Doubtfire type of joke?
- Sorry babe, the position has been filled.

I have noticed a smile on Mary's and Monique's faces. Those bitches are really messing up with me big time.

- OK, OK, I got the joke blah blah blah ... let's move, where is the office?

CHAPTER FOUR
Let's get ready to rumble

The office space on the 7th floor was very well organized. It wasn't made of glass as the outside of the building, thank God! We went straight to my office. It was so great with an astonishing view of palm trees and flower fields. Spacious and accommodating at the same time, it was equipped with a lovely crafted desk in the middle and many bookstands around. On the wall, there was a big TV just hanging like a painting.

On the desk I noticed a portable computer and a smartphone. I was a bit surprised that the room did not have few items.

- Mary dear, it gets very little to make me happy, you should know that by now. Would it be possible to have a mini-fridge in here? Oh! wait … will I get fat in this world too?
- Yes and yes you will, she answered.
- In that case add a treadmill as well. Preferably with

a phone attached to it. I have the greatest ideas when I work out.

- No problem. They will be ready tomorrow. Now let's get started. I have prepared all the bios of the people you will work on. All are on the computer. Plus you will be able to watch some of the programs on TV as I made a selection of the lowest of the low.

- Thanks Mary, You're the best.

Mary and Monique left the office and I could have some piece of quiet and not to think for a moment. I sat in my big leather armchair. I spun around once and looked at the view from the windows. I felt calmness coming onto me. I was missing this feeling for quite a long time. I never thought peace and quiet would bring something good, just opposite.

- Miss Joan, wake up.

I have opened my eyes and Monique was standing right beside me. I must have dosed off for a moment.

- Hey Mon, I can call you Mon, right? You can call me Joan.
- Of course, Joan! Mon is fine. I have brought you lunch.
- Lunch in the office? No way, I am not like that.
- Fresh salad, and for main course, steamed fish covered in caviar sauce.

That sounded familiar and I have almost felt the taste

of my favorite New York restaurant. What the hell…!

- Bring it Mon. I'll be happy to have it.

Food was fabulously prepared, delivered and was a pure joy to eat. It took me some time to finish it as I didn't want to end it so fast.

Afterwards I turned on the TV. Mosaic of windows showed up with various shows playing. I have chosen the one that seemed not so bad to the eye.

TV started to play episode of the show "Divas without the Voices". Short introduction at the beginning explained to me that this is some sort of comeback show for music divas from the past.

Announcer said:

In this fabulous divalicious episode we will meet once "white chick" from the Old York City with magnificent voice. America's End Sweetheart: Marey Krey. After marvelous career few decades ago, when people loved her voice and her fantastic personality she is now diva without a voice. She is kinda white diva who went "black and Waco" and makes fantastic music nobody wants to listen and buy … Let's welcome Marey Krey.

Hahaha… It does not sound so bad. Of course it's not high quality program but it seems funny. I wonder what comes next.

In this episode Marey will meet with another forgotten singer

Jeannette Jenkinson who was popular once, but unfortunate tour of events totally changed her career for the worse. Will those divas make a spectacular return? That is the main theme for upcoming season. Our team of experts will guide our stars of the past how to become once again women on top of the world.

He continued:
Let's meet our panel of experts. Fantastic one in a million Farthashian Family ... and one of the best rappers on the planet Lamey East.

Holly crap, it's that bimbo from the billboard, vagina face with enormous butt. But who the fuck is that Lamey? By looking at his deformed face and behavior, I can honestly say he is a morooooon right now.

Lamey stood up and started to cheer the crowd in the audience, like a monkey on drugs.

Yeah bitches, I am Lamey East, the best motherfucker rapper on the planet. On my concerts even crippled people on wheelchairs must stand up. Marey, Jeannette, I will show you how to do it ... You will be on the Edge of heaven soon ... everybody will love you like they love me ... yeahhhhh whoooo hhhaaaaaa.

Yeah right, like this is going to happen. What kind of moron would buy his records anyways? I think I will spare those babes some troubles and invite them to my show here on PTS. Maybe there is a hope for them after all.

I took a note on the computer about those fallen stars

with the suggestions for the meeting on my talk show. Jeez I forgot even to ask Mary what is the name of this show I am hosting. But it's a first day here so I think I have more time.

I took a break from watching and went for a short walk in the office. I thought introducing myself to other people on the show would be a good idea.

I have no idea how it could be possible but people working at PTS were happy. All smiling and polite. Is this just a cover or this place is a heaven?

The office space was very well organized. There was a huge wall in between with approximately 20 TVs running different channels simultaneously on both sides so everyone could see it.

Noticeable office appeared when I crossed by desks of the newsroom. The name at the entrance had Mandy Williamson on it. They were wide open I have knocked, do'h it's obvious. People remember to knock it may save you an unnecessary heart attack or marriage.

Anyways, Mandy was on the phone talking to someone. She was a fabulous looking black woman with bright smile on the face and freaking number of wigs around the desk. She was laughing many times during conversation. She had noticed me, gave me a huge smile and waved. Her conversation finished shortly afterwards.

- How you doin' babe. You look hot …. and who the hell are you? I am just kidding.
- Joan here, I am the new host of the celebrity talk show.
- What's the name of the show?

Ooops! I should have asked for that earlier. Had to make up some name so here it goes.

- It's "Joan is ON".
- Catchy, but I think it's a different name. I am Mandy Williamson and I am a co-host of the new show "How you doin' with Joan and Mandy".

Mandy started to laugh out loud. I got a bit embarrassed but started to laugh with her. What else could I do? I am the person who easily laughs at herself.
- OK Mandy, You got me. I made the name just now. It's my first day here.

- Not a problem. I guess I know a little bit more than you do.
- I have only watched short previews of some dummy show you probably heard about. It's "Divas without the Voices". I still need to get more information on what is going on in here.
- I am telling you now Joan, with two of us together it's going to be out of this world. You will see.

CHAPTER FIVE
How can we make it work?

After some laughs with Mandy we decided to have a dinner in the restaurant somewhere in the city. As I had no idea where to go, it was up to Mandy to choose the place. We took the limo that drove me here in the morning and went to the city.

Hollywood-end was just a part of the city known here as Lost Angels. We started our ride at 6 p.m. and it was getting a little bit darker. The city looked much better at night as there were so many flashing buildings, billboards and other type of lights. Mandy have chosen "The Supper Room" restaurant in Santa Magdalena near the ocean and the beach. We had a table booked for 8 p.m.

Before arrival, we took a short walk near the beach. We have been walking for about 30 minutes and I enjoyed the scenery very much. I haven't seen such a beautiful sunset in a long time. It was relaxing experience and good start to a fabulous evening with my new pal Mandy.

Restaurant was located in the hotel. It was quite nice place. We had reservation for a nice table with little bit more privacy than the others.

Mandy assured me that food served there is really high quality and is very tasty. During our walk on the beach she already described the best dish she had there, an Indian dish named "Undhiyu".

As I am always up for good food, I waited with anticipation to get a bite I never had before in my life.

We sat at our table.

- So Joan. We're going to be hosting a new show on PTS. From what I know, we got the best time slot and the best days. Are you happy to have your own show?

- Mandy dear, this experience is not new to me. I already had so many talk shows in the past on so many TV networks, I hardly remember them all.

- You are not that old. You are 35–40 years old. How many jobs could you have?

- Believe me I had plenty. I have sharp tongue and I say what I think, even if it is inappropriate. In most cases people laugh out loud. Basically I say things that people are afraid to say. Can you live with that?

❊ ❊ ❊

- How you doin' babe? I am pretty much the same. Love people and interact with them. I hate bad taste and love wigs.

- Say what?

- Wigs darling. Every day new shoes, new dress, new wig ... Hush, Hush ... Who cares! I want to feel fabulous darling. I do not much care what others say about me. But have noticed other people care what I say about them. Strange isn't it?

Mandy was talking and talking and talking about herself for the next 20 minutes or so. I thought I am mother "talker" but hey, she wins this round.

The main course arrived to our table and, for a second, I thought, "Thank You Lord for this fabulous food and closing mouth of my co-host for awhile".

Do not understand me wrong. I already started to like Mandy very much. She has a drive and she is very funny to look at. Her face has constant smile written on. If I only knew such people in the past, my life would have been even funnier.

Back to the food. It was a fierce mix of flavors that came from seasonal vegetables and special combination of herbs and spices. As a bonus, we got deep-fried Indian bread. The taste was explosive. If you ever had Indian food in your life, you know what I am talking about. But it was a pleasure to eat. It left me with happy feeling. Mandy enjoyed her food too. It wasn't the first time she ate it here so it was not such a surprise to her as it was to me.

After a while we have ordered something sweet to loosen up some spices in our bellies as they were on fire.

- Joan, do not get me wrong or anything. Are you single sweetheart?

- Yes, I am Mandy. I was in relationship before but it suddenly ended. I do not want to talk about it, forgive me.

- Oh no! Joan it's your business. I was wondering if we could go on some sort of vacation and get to know one another better. We could prepare some ideas for our show that starts in a month.

- That's a fabulous idea. Where do you think we could go this time of the year?

- It might seems crazy but have you ever been to Croatia, Joan?

- Croatia? Where is that? Never heard of it.

- It's in Europe, Mediterranean Sea. If you never been there, you must see it for yourself. You will love this place.

※ ※ ※

- Sure! Let's go to Croatia.

I was a bit skeptical about this vacation thing, but agreed to Mandy's proposal. She said she will arrange everything.

The evening was approaching its end. We chatted for an hour or so, and decided to call the night. We took the limo to get back to our homes. I dropped Mandy at her mansion near the beach and took a further ride to Mary's home.

CHAPTER SIX
The Insider

Next day I woke up after midday. I do not know why, but I felt tired and overwhelmed by all these meetings yesterday. I turned to another side of the bed and noticed Max sleeping with me. I could always count on my furry buddy to warm my heart. I gently started to pet his head and ears. He opened his right eye and yawned at my face. Can you imagine something more beautiful than this? We spent next 10 minutes cuddling and having fun. I love this new body thing. I always hated all my aches and pains. I always wanted to be young, beautiful and healthy. Well who wouldn't? Never thought I could get it back.

I went downstairs in search of Mary. This time I found her in the kitchen. She was making fresh coffee. Mhmmm what a smell! Love it.

- Joan so good to see you. How was yesterday. Did you have fun? Met anyone special?

※ ※ ※

- Mary, I had a blast. I met my co-host you didn't tell me about, Mandy Williamson. She's one crazy broad, just like me. I think we will get along just fine.

- Good to hear that. Have you made any plans? Sorry dear, I forgot to tell you more about the show before you met her. I hope you did not make fool of yourself. Joan is ON ….

-Mary, Mary how funny you are. Hahaha ….

Do not make fun of me girl. Next time I will show you my claws.

It was a nice afternoon. Sun was shining and leaves on the surrounding trees were humming beautifully. Such a nice feeling. I prepared myself coffee too and went with Mary to the outside terrace.

- Mary, I have decided to go with Mandy on a vacation. She thought it would be good idea to get to know one another and plan the show.

- That's a marvelous idea! But we should also discuss tactics for us staying here. Do you have any thoughts on that?

- I have a plan but it needs a little research before I let you know. It should clear up very soon. You will be the first to get the news.

Having said that I thought it would be a good idea to

put Monique to use. During yesterday's conversation with Mandy, it came to my attention that Monique is a flirty perfectionist, not only glamorous but brainy too. She could be perfect for the job I am about to reveal. She has been working with PTS for quite awhile and always delivered fantastic results. Whenever she was asked to do something she came with first class ideas. That's what I heard. I do not know the broad but that's what Mandy told me. All I know is she has a twisted taste of humor.

I got myself ready and went to work. On the way to the office, I have browsed some websites and researched on Farthashians. They will be my primary target, and Monique will help me get them off the air for good. You probably think that it is too good to be true. Watch few episodes and you will know that they are nobody without smart people that surround them. Having someone trusted and way smarter than them will give me access to inside world of Farthashians's emptiness.

I reached office at the lunch time. Many people left the place to get short break from watching flickering TVs and computer screens. I went straight to my office to read some more.

After awhile Mandy knocked on my door.

- How you doin' girl?
- Right now, very well, thank you very much. Slept till noon. It was a night to remember, for sure.
- Yes it was fun, we must do it more often and with

the upcoming 2 weeks of work freedom we will.

- Sounds about right!

It was a good time to share my plans for Monique with Mandy. As she told me so many good things about her, she should be interested in a plan I have prepared for her.

- Mandy, with us having fun at the sea side, we should use Monique's skills to infiltrate Farthashians. She's a smart girl and should be able to do it without any special problems, I think.

- It may be a good idea. I have heard Sin, the famous Farthashian, is big spender and is shopping constantly on Rodeo Road. I'll let Monique know our plans and prepare her departure.

- Maybe we should meet first, I mean three of us. I have few ideas of my own.

Mandy grabbed her handset and instantly called Monique, asking her to come by the office. Personally I thought infiltration should start with following Farthashians habits day by day, starting with shopping, gym, fitness, spa and restaurants.

When Monique arrived, we asked her to trace all Farthashians's moves. Gave her specifics on how to behave and what should be the primary target for evaluation. Mon seemed to be excited about such activity as it was kind of new to her.

Everything seems to be covered. Now we can go with peace of mind. Can we?

CHAPTER SEVEN
Before we fly away

Before departure, I decided to get some clothes and prepare myself for the upcoming vacation. Never liked to spend money but woman got to do what she got to do. But this vacation is rather special. I am dead and having time of my afterlife? Honestly it doesn't even seem like afterlife. It's like an alternate universe or something with the same ups and downs we have had on Earth.

I feel way different though. Am I losing myself? What happened to my jokes? Why the fuck am I so polite and appropriate. I was bold bitchy and sometimes crazy weird. I liked my old self. I cannot forget it and become another "Bold and Beautiful" character type of woman. Do not get me wrong, I remember few tough broads on this series but I am different.

I have asked Monique to take some time off work and show me around the shops they have in the city. I want to buy something light and colorful, maybe some jewelry. I wonder if they have something similar to my collection.

Monique showed up fresh and happy .We took a car and went to the city. I am not a fan of the malls but in the case of the one Mon took me to I can make an exception. It wasn't something like we could find in our world. All shops were inviting, easy to access and without special restrictions and boundaries. Mary gave me a credit card earlier with no idea of its limit. I do not know if I could have some fun with it. Maybe I will, you only live once. OK twice :). I saw a family wondering and looking at things. Kids who were accompanying their mother were kind of sad and looking at surrounding things like something they would love to have.

Without any hesitation I approached them. Mother was kind of surprised and scared. Good thing, I was not looking like 81 used up broad without make-up. That would scare hell out of her and poor kids.

I had a short chat with her. She came out to be very friendly and hard working mother of six. Yes, six kids! I always admired women who can do it on her own so many things. Her name was Ksav and she was working all around Hollywood-end as a cleaning lady. Unfortunately for her she wasn't paid well and always was used by greedy rich people.

I always liked to make people happy. I know buying things is not always a good idea, because best things in life are free like Luther Vandross used to sing. Luther he is dead I think. Maybe he's somewhere in the city. Anyways .... I am what I am. Buying presents for my grandson was a pure pleasure. I couldn't resist. Seeing people happy and enjoying themselves is very rewarding.

In case of this family, it was even better. After a short chat, Ksav told me that she worked for many famous people in the neighborhood. Guess who one of the clients was. Yes, you are correct. Farthashians! It couldn't get any better. I think we will become best friends from now on, really close friends.

I splurged lots of cash on Ksav's kids. Bought them all necessities and some things they wouldn't even think of buying because of the price.

It was fun meeting. I asked Ksav to come tonight for a dinner so we could get to know one another better. I promised to prepare food myself. Yeah right, me cooking. Thank you beautiful mall for having restaurant which delivers. I will prepare something to drink as I do not want to lie or anything [wink].

Mon started to look at me a little bit different from now on. Hell knows why. I hope it's not love. But she was kind of sexy babe. OMG! What am I saying? Or maybe.

We finally went to shop for some clothes for myself. It didn't take us forever to find a very cute shop that had dresses I wouldn't mind put on my ass. I am not that picky as you may think. Yeah I know what you thought. Apologize. Just kidding, I wouldn't hear you say it anyways.

After 2 hours of shopping and trying on many, many things I was finally satisfied with the purchases. Do not get it wrong. You have to keep economy moving even in afterlife.

When I arrived home Max was already waiting for me. I took my bags full of clothes and went to check them out once again in my bedroom. Max went after me and jumped on the bed and started to look at me with strange look he never gave me before.

I love fur and couldn't resist buying one in the store this time. It was such a gorgeous scarf in light color that would be a perfect addition to a cold evening during our vacation.

- You bitch. How dare you wear that?

I heard male voice saying that but couldn't locate anyone beside me and Max.

- Who said that, I replied.
- You must be fucking insane. Would you fucking wear me on your fucking neck, bitch?

I looked at Max and all my wrinkles showed up on my face.

※ ※ ※

- Max you can talk.
- No shit, Joan.
- Why didn't you say anything before?
- It was difficult for me to resist saying something earlier today, but your hands were doing such a good job on me so I didn't want you to stop

- Holly shit, you are one fucking pervert.

- D'oh, with all your fucking swears and dirty jokes my vocabulary is slightly altered. But after these years at least we share the same sense of humor. Don't even say that you are not taking me on your Croatian trip. Mary is fine broad, but I need some action with European bitches.

- OMG! It's hard for me to comprehend. What is happening right now?
- OK, let's analyze. You are fucking dead, kicked the bucket few days ago, looking like 40-something sexy babe. You are here with talking dog in a place called Hollywood-end. Shit, really. Wake up Sista. Anything is possible.

I was extremely surprised. I didn't know what to answer. I have noticed Max was giving me an "evil" wink. OMG! I raised a Satan. Lord Heeeeeeelp!

CHAPTER EIGHT
Spies 'r' Us

It took me awhile to put myself together after Max's reveal, but I had to. I have a dinner to prepare and knowing my talent for cooking I need some magic or one fine helping hand to make food eatable.

I asked Monique to come by and help me out with grocery shopping and preparation. My second day here and still not quite know what and where is located. You wouldn't too.

3 p.m. was approaching very fast, we didn't want to waste any more time by going to any fancy schmancy deli. Monique chose Meli Deli located nearby. It was not big, but what it had inside really surprised me in a good way.

This amazing deli shop had four lanes with selections of fruits and veggies, many varieties of meats, cakes and sweets, dairy products. There was also a place with fresh bouquets of gorgeous looking flowers. I was in deli heaven. Maybe because I haven't been avid grocery shopper in my past and haven't experienced such amazing organization and presentation of daily use products.

As Max already sent me his greetings with bitches and tones of fuck at home, I decided to go with something vegetarian for tonight's meeting.

We took trollies and went to the first lane of deli. They had massive selection of fruits and vegetables. They looked so fresh as if they were delivered from the garden earlier today.

For me it was really a strange feeling. I was used to buying clothes, jewelry, cosmetics, but never food. It's always been there and I wouldn't have to worry to buy anything at least for home, restaurants are different scenario.

Kudos to Monique. That broad was so much better in so many areas than me. She took a command of the trollies and started to stuff it with delicious looking food – aubergine, tomatoes, spinach, ricotta cheese, parmegiano regiano, wine, freshly baked bread, kiwis, grapefruit, melon, wine, nuts, olive oil, honey and mustard. She even grabbed a butterscotch cake on the way out of food sections. Let's hope she knows how to prepare all these ingredients into something special. I do not have a session of "Dancing without the stars" in the bathroom afterwards.

※ ※ ※

At the exit we grabbed a couple of admirable nosegay flowers to sweeten the meeting.

City was not crowded even in our outskirts, which was such a relief. It took us maybe 10 minutes to get back home. Mary greeted us at the door with a warm and honest smile. I wish people be that way in real life.

There was no time to waste. Ksav was supposed to come at 6 p.m. and I have asked Mandy to be here a bit earlier so I could let her know all the findings and prepare strategy.

Off to the kitchen. Mon took over the control there, grabbed aubergine and started to fill it with cheese goodness, spinach, etc.

- You know Joan I am not a master-chef. During our ride I have found tasty recipe on ccdgoodfood.com website. Everything is under control. Tonight we will serve aubergine rolls with spinach and ricotta plus red wine, fruit salad and butterscotch cake to arrive in luscious heaven by the end of the evening.

- Oh darling. I wish I knew what you just said. I haven't eaten any of these. Let's hope it's going to be good.

- Keep your pants on. It will blow your taste buds.

I took a minute or maybe two to step off the kitchen

and went to the bedroom to prepare myself. Max was stretching his butt on my pillow. When he noticed me, he rolled back to look at me and farted in progress.

- What a fuck did you just do? Are you insane? Pillow, seriously?

I was waiting for an answer and I didn't get it. Instead, Max stood up on his feet and started to frisk. Was I hallucinating? Grimace on my face appeared and I started to evaluate what happened earlier.

- What was I thinking? Dogs can't talk.

I lay down near Max and gave him a big kiss on his head, then looked and his sweet face. He smiled and ...

- BOOOOOO ... Oh yeah baby do it again and again.

Devious dog started to laugh out loud at me. Can you fucking believe it?

- Holly molly, you got me again. Stop doing this or ...
- Or what? You'll love me, just that way I am and you will not do anything MOTHER!

- Do not be so sure babe. From now on bed is off the limit. You can take this smelly pillow with you and move your ass down. NOW!

I grabbed the dress I bought in the morning and went

to the bathroom.

When I came down, Mandy was already there.

- How you doin' darling. You like my new wig? Wanna feel it? Kidding!
- Mandy what's up girl! Looking flawless as always.
- Are you coming onto me sweetie pie? started to laugh.
- Do not flatter yourself, you sexy thing. Hahaha...

I like Mandy so much already, she is really one funny babe. Whenever I see her, she puts smile on my face. I always loved that kind of quality in people.

- Is Ksav already yet? You will like her Mandy. She is such a wonderful human being. Six kids, working her way up to the top one step at the time.

- How did you meet her Joan? You just came here few days ago.
- We went shopping earlier and found our "insider" in shopping mall.
- Insider? What do you mean by that?

- Ksav is a cleaning lady to the "stars". With her on our side we could have unlimited access and fresh information from the front line. She is now lending her services to Farthashians. Does that ring a bell? For me it does. What we know now is really limited to the creepy but unfortunately popular show "Meet the Farthashians". They want us believe that what we see is true. I want to get inside and get all the dirt on them, shame them on national TV and hopefully remove from the public eye.

- Jeez Joan, You sound like a "buzzed" and it's freaking me out a little bit. But I think we can work with that, after our vacation of course.

- Of course dear. Monique will take over for the time of our vacation. I have a plan for her. It may not be glamorous thing to do, but she will spy on Sin Farthashian while we're gone.

- Interesting approach. It may be very good idea Joan. Farthashians behind of behind the scenes. Hahaha….

- Something like that, I have seen how they are behaving on the show and it gets me suspicious enough to think that something is going on there, they do not want us to see and know. Oh! I hear the bell ring. It must be Ksav. Look at the clock Mandy. She's up to the minute, punctual as the atomic clock.

I rushed to the door to greet our new best friend without any hesitation. While walking to the entrance I passed by Mary. Asked her kindly to join us in the living room and went to get Ksav.

Opened the door and was blown away. She looked so sublime and fresh.

* * *

-Ksav, so great to see you again. You look fabulous.
-Good Evening Joan. Thank you. It's because of you, this dress looks even better in the evening lights.
- Come on, please get inside. Mandy is already here as well as Monique, you already know her and Mary, she is my guide to everything in Hollywood-end.

I grabbed Ksav's hand and we went straight to the living room. I only hoped that food prepared by Monique will be eatable and enjoyable to all guests. When we arrived to the living room I have noticed that Monique left probably to see if the food is ready in the kitchen.

- Mary, Mandy, this is Ksav.
- Nice to meet you Ksav. I am Mandy, co-host of the show. How you doin' with Joan and Mandy.
- Never heard of it. I am so sorry.
- Darling, It's brand new. Episode one will air in a month or so. Nothing to be sorry about. Oh my God, you are so cute. You look so gorgeous in that dress, and your hair, that is divalicious.
- Thank you so much. It's so very kind of you. Just to let you know it's a wig I am wearing.

- Say what?
- A wig.
- Wiggy Wiggy Wig Wig Whack?
- Wiggy Wiggy Whack, best of luck.
- Oh my God. I love you already. We are so n'sync. I am wig addict myself. Have a wig for each day. And you even know special wig maniac greeting. That is so

awesome. I have never met anyone in Hollywood-end who's the member of Wiggy Whack club. Oh Joan! Joan ... come on over here.

- Be right back. I'll see what is happening with our food. Please enjoy yourselves for a while. Like Barbra used to say 'talk among yourselves' ... hahaha...

Smell from the kitchen was already discoverable, very tasty scent to be honest. Mon really outdid herself with the food this time. When I arrived at the kitchen, everything was beautifully organized and prepared for serving.

As all my guests already arrived, we took everything into the dining room. You may be surprised to see me serving. I am surprised too. Now you see what death can do for you. It will change you the way you would never think is possible.

- Girls everything is ready. Please come to the dining room.
- Joan, smell is wonderful. What did you do for us?

- Ok I wanna be straight with all of you. I am a bad cook. I can boil water, but that wouldn't be a good idea for today's meeting. Things you are about to eat were prepared by wonderful Monique. I said earlier that this dinner will be my personal work. I really wanted to do it for you, really. I even took Mon shopping and we both selected all of these especially for you.

- Honey it's wonderful the way it is. I sincerely hope there is more than that. You are a sweetie, so there must be something delightful for the dessert.

- Mandy dear, of course there is. But this surprise will leave for next hour.
- Ksav, Mandy, Mary and Monique. Thank you for being here with me tonight. I have never expected to meet so many beautiful "inside" people in my first days being here.

I saw instant smiles on all faces sitting right beside me and it brought me so many memories of my family dinners. I always loved to have people that I could really love and care for ones close to me. I could never comprehend people who abandoned their kids. I do not mean like small children. Parents in most cases forget about their kids when they have their own families. Visiting only for special occasions, not knowing what is going on in their lives. I wasn't one of them and sincerely hope there are other parents who think of their kids every day. I couldn't leave home and have a good time without calling my daughter first in the morning. It was like a ritual for me. Do not think it's crazy. If you do think, it's improper behavior, stop what you're doing right now. I mean it. Take a phone and call your kids. Life goes pretty fast. Do not let it pass you by. I am getting emotional in my brain. Shit, how is this even possible, no time for this right now. We have to get rid of celeb dirt of this Hollywood-end shit hole.

※ ※ ※

My new friends were enjoying their food and smiling at one another. Once again, huge kudos to Mon. She literally saved my ass.

- Ladies, Ladies. I would like to say something. I am really glad to see around me strong women who know how to handle tough situations in their lives. I do not know what you think about celebrities in this town, but with all the info I have gathered today, I am sure you were used by them one way or the other. I do not want my planning to be a revenge or anything. I want to teach them a lesson, they will never forget.

Ksav looked at me with an intriguing smile. I was sure she would be most interested in getting back at those talentless assholes. She got used to clean their daily dirt from the floors. Now it's time to get the dirt out for the world to see.

- Joan. You were so thoughtful for me and my kids. I knew there is something special in your eyes, minute I saw you in the mall. You seem like from another world.

No shit Ksav. I kicked a bucket few days ago, so it may seem like it.

- I love honest people and you seem to be one of them. Do not treat all of this as a scheme to use you. OK, maybe a little but it was total coincidence when I met you today.

- Ksav laughed loud at me. I love your honesty. I

admire straightforward people. No need to hide anything as sooner or later everything will see the light of day.

- I like you even more for saying that. Straightforward it my middle name. Where I come from people hated me for saying things, other people wanted to say, but were afraid to.

- Joan darling, let Mandy say something. I am the co-host you know, right? Let me do the talking for a change.

- Yes my queen of talking. Go ahead.

- OK where to start. You all look so beautiful tonight. It's a pleasure to be in your company. Joan, thank you for organizing this "house party event".

- That's all? This is impossible. I would expect more from you.

- It's your evening darling. I am a classy woman and will not take the spotlight at this time.

- Thanks Mandy. Is surprise your middle name?

I briefly laughed and looked around. I have noticed Max coming into the dining room. Holly crap, all I need now is this pervert to do the talking.

- Sorry ladies. Be right back.

※ ※ ※

I went to the corridor and closed the door to the dining room as I didn't want the ladies to hear me talking to the dog. They would totally think I am really "SPECIAL".

- Max where are you going. No dogs allowed. This is all women party.
- Joan, do not be a bore. Let me in and snuggle around those fab babes. I have good ideas too. Sooner you tell me what you're planning the better.

- I am not planning anything.

- How dare you lying to your beloved pup. I overheard your conversation with Mary, so cut the crap and let me in. I know stuff. I have been here before you and let me tell you babe, you will need me.

- OK. Come on in but please shut the fuck up in front of my girls.

I have opened the door and Max started to walk. He turned his head and whispered.

- I will just lick their feet. I love fresh fingers for dinner. Hauuuuuu...

- You motherf※※※※.

Max started to playfully move his tail and entered the room.

* * *

- Girls, this is my dog Max. He really wants to meet you.

- He told you that?

- Yes Mandy. He is one fucking pervert. He also told me that he's into your feet so beware.

Ladies started to laugh hard, myself included. I have only noticed the look on Max's face saying "bitch". No wonder I always loved him. We are so in sync.

- OK, now it's time to prepare our moves for upcoming weeks. Mon already knows what's her assignment. Follow Sin Farthashian in the city and get to know what she does on daily basis. Ksav dear, do you have any ideas honey?

- Actually I do have some thoughts. Week ago I have overheard that Sin is in search of new assistant. She already had few meetings but without results. She is using "SHeWood" agency. Mon you could at least to try to get an appointment. Who knows, maybe this would be a better idea than following Sin throughout the city.

- Ksav, that is a splendid idea! We would have two insiders then. Mary, can you please set up a meeting for Monique. Myself, Mandy and Max are leaving tomorrow for a short vacation. We will be in touch with all of you, so not to worry in advance.

When I said Max is going with us, he was about to lick Mandy's fingers. He raised his head and pulled back his nasty tongue.

Everything seemed to be taken care of. Ladies were excited with their upcoming activities and so was I with the next two weeks of pure hopefully uninterrupted holidays.

CHAPTER NINE
Let's Fly Away

I was really excited about our trip. I have travelled the world before. Been to Europe and Asia in my life many times, but Croatia was the land I have never heard of nor been to. Geography was not my thing for sure, if you know me you already know that. I am smarter than 5th graders for sure. I had a small "Joan's empire" for God sake. My legacy will be strong for years to come and I am proud of myself to achieve so much in my past lifetime. I am getting emotional again. Shit. I have to stop going back with memories as it is very hard to leave everything behind without any way back. I only hope we will meet again someday soon. It is possible. I have my Max back. Let's get back to business, that is enough. Memory lane is closed for next two weeks.

Last night was for sure to remember. I had a lot of fun and all my plans seemed to be taken care of, and on the right path to success. I have packed all the clothes bought yesterday. Yes you are correct, fur scarf included. I have to tease my beloved dog a little bit more.

Mandy and myself decided to meet at the airport. I was really pleased that this was not direct journey. We have a connecting flight from London to Pula and then we're getting a car and driving to Rabac. That sounds exciting.

Max was hysterical yet happy. He told me earlier what he would like to take, so I added his extra belongings to my luggage.

Car was waiting for us. I gave a big kiss to Mary and said everything will be alright. Max jumped on the back seat and looked at me. I could read him very good, even when, I didn't know he could talk. His expressions were always faultless. Right now he was saying "European bitches yeaaaah".

I jumped into the car. Who would have ever thought me "JUMPING"? That is amazing, I feel so good and full of energy.

Ride to LAXXX airport was taking forever. I thought that driving at this time of day would not be an issue. Unfortunately I was wrong. Highway was full of cars. Driver told me that it will take us at least an hour to get there.
I took my laptop out of the bag and started to watch an episode from "Meet the Farthashians".

It's not something I would watch to spend some good time, but I have to know my enemies better. I am not going to bother you with what I just saw. It was hideous and plain dumb. It was not even funny.

I used to have my little (ok not little) reality TV stunt with my daughter. At least we wanted it to be funny and gave people some good laughs while watching TV. But this? What the fuck is this. I wonder how people could be interested in other people's empty and evident bullshit, without rhyme and reason.

I want to go to the hairdresser I wonder, what my lovely Lamey will say. OMG. Do you think my ass needs an adjustment. I think I need a gold lavatory. Yes Lamey, I will add pearls too.

OMG! WTF is more appropriate for this crap. Add his picture in front of you while taking dump, you will do it much faster.

There was one thing that interested me though. Sin, the most recognized of Farthashians, was always giving the same facial expressions. Seemed a bit robotic, but hey maybe it's the way she is. Sometimes it is hard to distinguish what's real, especially by watching it on TV, don't you think?

- Miss Joan, we're at the destination. LAXXX is in front of us.
- That was fast. You said it would take us an hour to get here.

- That is correct. We have been driving for 75 minutes.

And now you know. Cut your TV habits. 75 minutes? Seriously? You are throwing out your life for something so absurd, dull, imbecilic and foolish pseudo entertainment. Sorry, it's not even entertainment, it's not even funny. Would you watch not so famous family doing not so fancy things? Shit maybe you would and maybe they would be more realistic than Farthashians. But you shouldn't. There are more fun things on TV than this, that I am sure about. If not TV, take your asses outside. There are plenty of things to see and enjoy in the world.

Mark, that was the name of the driver parked in front of the entrance to the terminal. I grabbed Max and my all-time favorite orange Hermmmessy bag and got out of the car.

- Mark, honey could you please help me with my bags. I am already hands-full with my furry friend and my handbag.
- Certainly. Where are we going? Mandy said she will wait for me in the lounge. I am not quite sure where it is. I'll just call her.

- Mandy girl, where are you?
- Joan darling, I am in the VIP lounge on the east side of the terminal. It's not so far away from the main entrance. You have to get through security check first.
-OK thanks babe, I will see you in a while.

* * *

As Mark overheard our conversation he took the bags, I took Max and we went for the security check. For a moment I thought: what the hell! I do not have any documents, passport. How the fuck am I going to pass by the security, yet get into the plane not having printed tickets either?

Security check was like out from the future. There was full body scanner. We had to enter the booth and stay there for few seconds. I have noticed display inside saying to put your hand on it. I did that with a little fear. That could easily cut my hand or shit like that.

By all means, nothing like that happened. I was greeted with Hello Joan and ticket came off the place just below the scanner. That was it. The booth opened and I was allowed to go further. A nice looking chap took my hand and helped me to get off with my bags. Turned back and waved to Mark.

I was informed that Mandy Williamson is waiting for me in the VIP lounge in the east side of the terminal.

You wouldn't believe what I saw. During our conversation, a driverless car arrived. Something similar you would expect to see on Earth like airports but this was like out of this world. I was asked to sit in one of two available places. Bags were taken to be loaded into the plane. Few buttons were pushed and we were on our way to the VIP lounge. How fantastic is that. Max was certainly enjoying himself as his mouth was wide open and happy expressions were only visible on his beautiful face. That made me feel so good. Within a few minutes we arrived at the lounge. Mandy noticed us and started to wave from the distance.

- Mandy darling. Why didn't you tell me about the airport? It's so out of this world.

- Darling. No kidding. How the hell did you get into the Hollywood-end? By foot?

- No honey, I fell from the sky.
- So you must have been using the airport then.

- Let's just say it was a little bit different departure and arrival than you think.

- OK darling. Sorry, I thought you knew. Enjoyed it?
- I certainly did enjoy.
- That's great, let's grab something to eat before the flight.

We went straight forward to the lounge, VIP. I rarely needed that kind of treatment but when it happened, I quite enjoyed it. LAXXX airport's VIP lounge was huge. It was not typical just sit and wait for your fucking plane area with grab-on food somewhere inside. It was more like an out of this world restaurant. Beautifully arranged tables with many colorful flowers on the sides, plus what's important the most, six stations with chefs serving variety of foods and drinks.

We have found ourselves great spot with spectacular view on the parked planes. I have noticed first they were way bigger than what we had in our world. I know you do not believe me. They were see-through at some point. Maybe I was hallucinating or maybe they have some sort of switches. Once you push them everything would become transparent. What the fuck I am babbling about, technology is not even my thing. Food, food, give some delicious and beautifully looking food.

I took a walk to see what was served in the lounge. Being a good food lover, I wanted to eat something very tasty. I was not disappointed. I went straight forward to chef who had fish dishes. I wanted to eat something fresh and not so heavy. Who knows what to expect on those flying machines. Maybe they have onboard shopping malls or water parks. I know it sounds insane but after seeing here all these advanced technologies, everything is possible.

I ordered steamed salmon and a salad, and will get to the drinks afterwards or on the plane. I do not think you are supposed to eat and drink at the same time. I couldn't forget about Max. He was in heaven already. After thinking for a second, I decided not to give him anything to eat. I do not want to push his metabolism and think about a load of crap on the plane few hours later.

Mandy was waving at me from the next station.

- Joan, Joan, come on over here – So I have heard.

❄ ❄ ❄

I was informed that my order will be delivered to the table when it's ready. I went in Mandy's direction to see what she was so anxious about. And there was it – a meringue cake. It was amazing looking and for sure tasty.

- Darling, do you see what I see?
- Yes Mandy, a cake is what I see.
- Are you kidding me babe. It's meringue cake filled with fantastic cream, dactyls, clone syrup, walnuts and God only knows what else. It will blow your head off, that's how good it is. I ate it few times but it is so hard to find.

- OK, OK. I will keep my head down and take one of these, please.

We were set up with the food and took our fat asses back to the table. I sincerely hope it was not microwaved but I have noticed chef was performing finishing touches on my dish. Taste buds beware.

- What are you having Mandy. I know the cake, but did you order anything else?

- You see my fab curves on this body. Of course darling. I am having a salad. Hahaha. I have to keep my fat ass in that size. Anything bigger will be tripled by the power of television. We already have one fat ass on TV and it ain't me, so let's keep it that way.

❄ ❄ ❄

Our orders arrived shortly and they were truly out of this world. It was crafted to perfection. Would you expect it from airport lounge? In most cases you have food buffet with something to grab, eat and get the hell out.

It took us awhile to enjoy this culinary art. Max was really pissed off at me because of no food policy on the plane. He should be happy for flying first class, as there are special animal seat zones that I was told. I have no idea how they really look like, but in few moments we will get on the plane and see.

We finished our dessert and I confirm, "This cake is to die for". It melts in your mouth like nothing I have ever tasted before. Pure joy, sweetness to the power of Hellllll yeah!!! Walnuts and dactyls add some extra flavors and this cream so silky. Can you imagine it? Sure you can, if you love sweets you already have a mouth full of saliva. Did I guess? Hahaha… Damn I still have it.

The time to get on the plane finally arrived. For me, it was uber exciting, because what I saw today surprised me very much. Don't do faces. You would be surprised too. Seeing something straight from science-fiction movie in somewhat more realistic way is mind-blowing. Remember "whyPhone?".

As I already mentioned, planes in here were huge. I have asked Mandy how many people can get on these. She replied that one thousand people can fly this thing at the time. Having a better budget to spend, she decided to get us first class cocoons. One of them would have extra space for accompanying animals. I really wanted to see this.

Driverless car arrived to VIP lounge and stopped in front of us. Voice from the loudspeaker started to talk:

Miss Mandy, Miss Joan, Mr. Max. Please take your seats. Departure is planned at 1500hrs.

Mr. Max, I repeated it out loud, looked at Max with "The Eye" and sort of surprised facial expression. He responded with the same, and said Hau Hau Hau ... Pheww... Buddy keep your skills only for us. We do not want "Max: The naughty dog" talk show anytime soon.

The ride was another pleasure. We rode on the special lanes but everything was visible. Right now I could truly enjoy the magnificence of this establishment. In short, lots of technology, tonnes of glass and colorful surroundings. Everything was a true pleasure to the eye – the shops, small coffee joints, souvenir booths. Everything was really well planned. I really enjoyed the ride. We stopped at the elevator. After a short moment, the door opened and we were allowed to get inside.

- Want to see something exciting Joan?
- Sure, why not.

✿ ✿ ✿

Mandy pushed the button on the elevator's control panel and everything suddenly became transparent. I yelled....

- Mandy, What the fuuuuuuuuuuckkkkkkkkkk...

Max took a dump. What was he thinking? It would not fall down you little asshole. I know, I know, he must have been surprised same way I was. It's first time for everything for us. Another thing we have in common here in Hollywood-end.

- Sorry Joan, you wanted me to push it and started to laugh.
- I know, now do the push up and help me clean this crap from the floor.

Few moments later we arrived at the plane entrance to the first class cocoons or whatever the hell they call it.

The door opened and we boarded the plane. I was blown away. Whole level had 13 cocoons. They were looking like small rooms the shape of a ball. We had one booked. Steward, with the name Mike placed on his sexy uniform, showed us where our places are located. He also said he's ready to help anytime we want. OK. I keep my mouth shut for awhile as I do not want to be called sexist bitch. But he was so adorable.

We arrived at our cocoon. Mandy was about to push the button, but I grabbed her hand.

※ ※ ※

- Are you sure what you're doing?
- Joan relax. I only want to open the door.

She turned her head in my direction and said in a creepy voice.

- Do I?
- Stop playing with me Mandy. Don't be a bitch.

Suddenly door opened and I was blown away once again. This cocoon had windows. Maybe not the ones you would expect from a normal plane. They were widescreens and you could see so much more detail from outside. The projection, as these couldn't be windows per say, was so real. Cocoons were located inside the plane after all. You could feel the realness coming from it and it felt amazingly scary. Two comfy sofa beds were present plus a section with snacks and drinks. Flowers, magazines, books, everything looked so sophisticated and high-end. Max found special place that was dedicated to accompanying animals. He jumped straight away on the bedding and flipped on his back.

Now it's time to relax and enjoy the flight. I wonder what Ksav and Monique are up to. I hope Mary did not forget to arrange the meeting with the agency. I will let her do the talking for awhile and keep the action going. Is that OK with you? Of course it is. You do not have any other choice. Do not put it down. OK, turn the page and let's go. It's page 70-something, do not give up on me now.

CHAPTER TEN
Conspiration

During the time Mandy and Joan had so much fun enjoying their food and novelties of this new world, I started to do her part of the job. Once Joan waved me goodbye and left for the fun-filled vacation, I called Monique straight away and asked her to come by the house.

An hour later Mon arrived and we began to scheme the way to get in to Farthashians's residence. Ksav couldn't help us more at this very moment as her cleaning appointment was made for the day after tomorrow. You may wonder how one lady could clean so much crap. I assure you right now she is 1 of 13 cleaning ladies who come to Farthashians two times per week to take care of all scrubbing, washing and dusting. She sure will help but, what is needed now is to get Monique inside.

This shouldn't be hard to achieve, but who knows

who Sin is looking for. Mon is very smart, sexy, intelligent and eloquent babe, but maybe having some of her qualities altered would help somehow. We will see how it goes.

You may think, yeah right it's so easy to become an assistant to someone famous. Answer to you. It's Hollywood-end and anything can happen whether you like it or not (I hope so). It sounded so cheesy. It's gonna be HARD. Better?

- Monique, I have called the agency and booked you an interview. It wasn't hard to get you that, but it's not all. This is the first stage where you will be asked many questions, and some tests will be performed. Everything will be taped. We have to be sure you look flawless. I am not worried about performance. I already know you are one of the best assistants PTS has. I did little research and think you are the best for this job. So, be natural yet professional during the taping and everything will be just fine.

- Mary, I suspect what Sin's requirements are. For sure she needs someone smarter and totally different than herself. She does not want some sort of an assistant to take over the spotlight. Nonetheless, I'll try to prepare and be perfect.

- Honey you don't have that much time, as the meeting with the agency is set up for today. We have to make it work as soon as possible. Joan is counting on us. Ksav will help of course, but to make it work you have to get inside. The lady I spoke to told me that Sin is very fast and they are giving feedback after maximum 2 days.

- Very good then, what time should we be ready?
- We have a meeting scheduled for 4 p.m.
- Great. Let's grab something to eat.

I took Monique to the kitchen and started to prepare the food. As it was sort of early afternoonish time of day, I went for something very not-so-fancy. Have you ever eaten a slice of bread with scrambled eggs inside? Garnished with tomatoes and mini cucumbers and topped with parmegiano cheese. Coffee of course was mandatory.

We talked for good 2 hours, and the time to get to the agency finally arrived. We still had some time so we decided to visit my good friend Kenny, who was an impersonator to the stars. He was really good. One of the best drag acts on the Hollywood-end soil. Having the ability to transform himself to practically any star was his huge advantage. Once I saw him like Cheer and Barbrrra. You probably do not know whom I am talking about. These two ladies are fabulous singers here in the city.

Kenny took over very fast. Thirty minutes later, her hair started to have the WOW factor. He also found great dress that looked like kind of stylish uniform. Mon was ready; she looked fierce yet professional. If Sin doesn't like her, we are going to have problems.

✿ ✿ ✿

I thanked Kenny, and hugged and kissed him goodbye. Mon was so happy with the new look that she hooked up with Kenny for the touch up next week. She got a very good impression on him, and they are on the road to become good friends. You know right, gays are the best friends for anyone.

We've been driving to SHeWood agency for some time now. It was usual traffic at this time of day. It's gonna be worse in few hours when people will be driving back home from work.

- Mon, are you excited? It's something new to you.
- Finally!!! I always wanted to have some action in my job. It's alright to be an assistant. What I hope it is to be more fun packed. Thank God for Joan. She brought some action into my world.

We have approached Marconi Street. I was opting to see office buildings; instead, it was typical residential area with nice-looking houses.

SHeWood agency was located in one of them. OK, I was a little bit worried about what to expect, but maybe it will be for our advantage – small house, small problems.

I parked nearby. Monique was a little bit stressed out and was saying to herself, "Everything will be OK, Everything will be OK...."

✿ ✿ ✿

I briefly smiled and laughed.

- Oh Mon, you are a sweetie. You want action but deep inside you are fragile like not-so-tough people. It's going to be fine. One way or another we will get in to the Farthashians house. Cheer up, relax and not to worry. Take a deep breath and go.

I slapped her butt while she was leaving the car. She turned back and laughed at me.

We have been punctual, the one thing they should appreciate in the assistant role from the start.

I tuned on the radio. I love country music and one of my all-time favorite song just came on. It was Tay Hardon with "Steam Leather". Woof, this guy is freaking hot and his voice melts my heart. I pulled back the car seat and started to dream on….

An hour or so later the door to the car opened and Monique entered. She was uber-excited but a bit agitated. Her face was sparkling.

- Mon, what happened? Tell me everything….
- That was a scary awesome experience. First, I had to wait for a while as the last interview was taking more time than expected. A hunky man at the reception greeted me. I received a questionnaire to fill. Just basic stuff, nothing to bore you with. That went quick. Then they asked me to come to an empty room. It looked a little bit bizarre. Why the hell would you interview

someone in a room full of mirrors, I thought. I didn't have to think twice. Sin must have been there watching from the back room or they have been monitoring me from all possible areas for future evaluation. Anyhow, I was greeted by a couple after few minutes. Woman in her late 20s and a bit older guy, maybe 30 something, started to ask me questions about Sin. What do I know about her, why would I like to work as her assistant, typical tidbits. So I answered, that I always admired people who are famous and keeping the eminence in focus of other people blah blah blah... .

- So what was their response? Did they like you?
- I do not know. They said they are Sin's managers and are looking for someone to help them out with appointment planning, some PR stuff and something similar. Previous assistant quit after a month. That's all was said. It got me a bit worried. Why on earth would she quit just after a month. Of course, they didn't wanted to explain it and I didn't wanted to be pushy and nosy, so I changed the subject to something different. Overall I think they were happy with what they saw and heard. There is a big chance we will hear from them.

- Pheew, that's good. Very good indeed. I wonder what our girls are up to in the air?

CHAPTER ELEVEN
In the Air

So far we have been enjoying our trip very much. Plane was something definitely to remember, but you already know it. Max was quietly sleeping on the couch; where else would you think he could put his furry ass on? Mandy was watching movies that were available on the plane's entertainment system and laughing from time to time. I was thrilled to see the surroundings on the plane.

We have been flying for some time and I was very curious to push the button that activates the monitors displaying the outside of the plane. I couldn't get myself to do it. Instead I went to the lobby near our cocoon. Of course it was not the lobby you would expect from the hotel, come on. It was big enough and I could get some shots to put myself into the coma or the state you wouldn't have to worry about a thing, especially with almost thousand people on board.

I noticed Mike flying around those cocoons, pleasing

everyone with whatever they wished for. I decided to see what he's up to. He was the kind of guy I would definitely snuggle with, if you know what I mean.

He had the face to remember, tough yet calm, not so long beard and moustache, and evenly placed eyes gave this hunk of man something that melted my legs. His uniform was very tight and you could practically see all his muscles and special areas. Did I mention his smile? This I think was his best feature. I know you do not believe me, you sick perverted women. Keep your fingers out of vagina right this minute!!! Not everything that makes man a man is located under his waist. OK I lied. I would fuck him if I had a change, happy now? You knew I will say it. You're getting to know me better every minute.

I was a bit buzzed off from the drinks. I didn't even bother to see how the economy class looks like on that plane. The area we were sitting at had only 13 cocoons. So, not so many people can be accommodated there. Where the rest 900 people are stuffed, I have no bloody idea. Maybe later I will ask Mike to give me a tour. For now I'll spend some time with my new favorite TV show "Spoiled and Dumb – Kids of Beverly Halls", whatever this shit is.

I lied down near Max, turned on the computer and started to watch the episode. Like Farthashians were empty as hell, these spoiled fucked-up brats were somehow even more obnoxious and one thing on your mind would be to kick their fucking asses as hard as possible.

I do not know if you are aware of this masterpiece, but let me give you the basics.

This show is about rich kids. They spend all time spending the money, screwing around, drinking and shit knows what else. I always wondered. Why the hell would God give stupid people so many privileges? They are not even good human beings. It's hard to say that spending money gives anything good to the society except keeping the economy running. All they think is romance, parties but nothing serious. This was something very disturbing to watch. It wasn't even funny at all, not entertaining, not creative. I'd rather see their butts working as hard as possible for those dollars they are spending without a thought on stuff they do not even need. Some of them claim to be well educated. Yeah right. You can wipe your fat asses with those diplomas. I may sound like Good Samaritan now. But if you know me, and I'm sure you do, otherwise you wouldn't have spent even a penny on this book, there are more important things in life. Am I right? Damn straight I am right.

I can't do it any longer. I slapped the laptop and decided to go for a walk. Max woke up and looked at me.

- Hey sista, keep it quiet. You're not giving me food and now you're not letting me sleep either. Jeez.
- Move your ass, we're going for a walk.

❊ ❊ ❊

Max jumped on his feet without a thought. Yeah right, you fake furry ass. Do not wake me up crap.

I noticed that Mandy waved to us and laughed hard. She had her headphones on. I hope she wasn't laughing at us talking.

I grabbed Max and we went out of our cocoon. Mike was walking in our direction and my legs began to shake.

- You have the hots for this fella?
- Oh shut up now. What do you think?
- Shake it off, shake it off … auuuuuuuuuu…

OK I admit I had the hots for him, but it was out of the question. I am professional, right? Mike approached us and said Hi.

- Mike, does flying first class include the tour of the plane. It's my first time flying. So far I enjoyed it very much. Could this be taken any further?
- Ms. Joan, what do you mean by further?

- Oh dear, don't get me wrong Mike. I'd love to see the place and Max could use the walk. I have heard over thousand people can fly on this thing. I wonder where they are accommodated. I love cocoon experience. But where the hell are the rest of the passengers sitting.

- No problem whatsoever. I am going to give you tour of the plane. You might be surprised by what you see.

※ ※ ※

- Dear Mike, Nothing can surprise me more than what I saw earlier today. Believe me.

We moved to the back of the first class area and entered the gate. Not star gate d'oh, different series. This was a special place where you could enter the other parts of the plane which had several floors of seats. First class floor was located at the top of the plane near the pilots. We used elevator to go down, no unnecessary buttons were pushed at this time. Few seconds later we arrived at the lounge with a small restaurant. You probably say. You are one fucked-up bitch, a restaurant right in your ass? How the fuck did you start the plane from the airport? I am calming you down my dear friend. These planes are not starting as the ones you know and use. This one simply moved up vertically and then flied smoothly without any issues and bumps. Simple, isn't it? Maybe someday in your lifetime you will be able to experience in your own skin.

Enough with the technobabble. The restaurant was pretty nice. It was not as sophisticated as on the airport, but pleasant enough. Economy class was looking quite fine, I haven't noticed people complaining, even better they were happy to be on board and enjoying the flight. I have no freaking idea, why people are so fucking happy here in this world. Is dead the solution to eternal happiness? I don't think so.

Short trip on board was enjoyable. I was predicting the outcome, as the start of this journey struck me hard in a somewhat good way. We have returned to our cocoon. On the way back I grabbed two slices of delicious-looking cheese cake for myself and Mandy.

There was an announcement made by the pilot that we're going to arrive in London in approximately 50 minutes. For a moment I thought, I love that kind of travel. I hated to fly several hours from coast to coast when I was alive. Few hours and we're on the other side of this world.

CHAPTER TWELVE
London by Night

Our flight to London was about to end. This flying experience was really something I will remember until the end of my afterlife. OK, it didn't sound right. Hell, whatever. For the whole time of our journey so far, Mandy was watching movies, like it was something she never did before. When she finished, I was told that it is the best way to see the movies that weren't released to the cinemas. First class passengers on international flights have early access to special movie library. Huge movie studios are preparing for the big premieres counting on influential and rich people to watch their productions and creating the buzz around them. Clever idea, I thought. I like to watch movie from time to time, but it's nothing extra special for me. New movies weren't exactly the thing I enjoyed most in the past. My movie taste was nothing extraordinary, starting with musicals and ending with various crazy things. I will not bore you with that, and you don't need to know everything about me.

※ ※ ※

Before the plane began to land I decided to push the "special" button. The view of London by night was magnificent. Our cocoon became transparent and we could enjoy the view the best possible. This was the place full of positive energy and centuries of history behind it. Blinking lights that came from the streets and buildings made me excited. I remember my show performed in the Scotland a few years ago. This was such a great experience. My memories started to come back. I think I will be able to trick this world and keep what's most precious to me for a long long time. That's good, as I do not want to forget my family. I know it's tough not having them around anymore, but they are so real in my memories. I have to have them forever.

Plane finally landed and we were able to move out of our fabulous place. Max was the most willing to leave the plane. He drank some water during the flight, so he must have wanted to piss on something British for a change. Damn dog.

- Honey, did we book a hotel?
- Yes Joan, not to worry. MarryOtt Hotel is where we stay for the 2 nights. Our plane to Croatia has departure scheduled for the day after tomorrow.

- Any plans Mandy? We have one full free day tomorrow. Maybe we could go to see a play in the theatre. London is very famous for its West End plays.
- I know darling. There is one fabulous establishment called Chocolate Factory where I have been once. Don't

worry, the plays are not based around chocolate. They have very nice restaurant so we could have two in one, good food and good show. What do you think?

- Marvelous darling. You are so prepared. I love your ideas so far.
- You know I am always open for a change "How you doin' with Mandy and Joan" if you know what I mean [wink]… Kidding.

We touched the ground with our feet and went to the terminal. I say fucking no to the elevators, NEVER, especially at the airport. Our bags already waited for us and a friendly looking, 50-something man greeted us with super sexy British accent "Good evening ladies" … Grrrrrr. Goosebumps came over me. I loved it. I have replied of course with a Hello and gave him a smile he will remember for a long time hopefully.

We took a taxi. I was totally impressed with Mandy; she knew what to do, where to go. WOW. So far this trip was nothing but perfect.

Airport was not located in the city center, so it took us awhile until we saw the historical part on London. Hotel was placed near River Thames with spectacular view on the Eye of London and Big Ben tower.

It was truly a gem. Building was old as almost everything in this location. OK, there were also a few new buildings but they only made it worse looking from an historical perspective.

※ ※ ※

When I entered the hotel I immediately felt at home. The decor and everything in between was so in my style. Another breathtaking experience awaits me for sure. While Mandy went to check us in, I sat in the lobby and enjoyed the view. Everything seemed so taken care of with high attention to detail. Furniture, flowers and colors were balanced to the perfection. Gorgeous-looking lamps hanging from the top looked like they were taken straight from the palace. I was so thrilled to see our room.

Our room was located on the second floor of the building. I took the stairs. I wouldn't expect anything fancy and technology advanced from this place, but I'd rather not risk it.

- Mandy, what's our room number?
- 201 darling. You will love it.
- From what I saw below in the lobby, I am quite sure I will.

I do not want to bore you with another description, how lovely and fancy it was. I am quite sure you have enough of it. In short, the room was perfect. I loved the terrace and the view from it the most. You could easily use Big Ben as your alarm clock and watch people having fun on the Eye of London while drinking your morning latte.

Mandy and I woke up the next day around 10 a.m. We didn't want to waste our precious time here, so we ordered breakfast to the room in advance. It arrived on scheduled time at 10:30 a.m.

Everything was very good, looked smokin' and healthy. The show we were planning to see was supposed to start at 6 p.m. so we had some spare time to do the sightseeing of nearby areas.

We dressed up quickly. Max was finally pleased as he ate so much last night and today altogether. He asked us to leave him alone, just not to close the terrace door in case shit happens.

I was OK with that as it would be crazy weird to go with a dog to the theatre with dinner included. I do not mind taking him wherever I go. See I took him on this trip. Some of the people wouldn't hesitate to throw the poor animals to the shelter house or the woods just to have a pleasant uninterrupted stay at some fucking spa or shit like that. You got to treat an animal like it is a part of your family dumbass. I always was an advocate for taking animals from the shelters instead of buying them. OK, I wear/wore the fur. Maybe I shouldn't, because it is wrong to use animals for this purpose. Shit, nobody's perfect, not even me. Give me a break. It's not a good time to discuss it now. Time to see the city.

You may think that weather in London is always bad with constant rain and foggy atmosphere. That is so not true. There is at least one day with beautiful sky, sun that warms your skin and people walking like it was 40 degrees heat. I was really surprised to see so many people wearing only shirts and short pants whenever sun came up on the sky. They must have needed it so much, poor things.

The show we were about to see, called "Not So Terrible Advice", was something I was eager to experience from the first row. Mandy told me that the show is quite popular because of very talented and well-known cast. One guy from this show seemed familiar. His name was Scotty Fakula. This world is weird. So many similarities, you may even think that it is an exact copy of ours, maybe with little changes somewhere here and there.

I always loved extraordinary things, crafted to perfection, one of the kind. London is such a place with all that in common. Before we went to watch this play, I wanted to walk on the famous streets. Fuck, now I can walk and it does not hurt like a bitch. Even better, I can speak without any problems maybe even if I meet someone. I eagerly looked at the Eye of London. I wasn't quite sure whether I wanted to ride on it or not. This time I will pass on this. As this city has so much entertainment to offer, the real entertainment I must say, it's really hard to find the best things and enjoy them during one day stay. We crossed to the other side of the River Thames, walked nearby the Big Ben and then went to the famous Piccadilly Circus. You know what's very close to that place. Yes, yes my biggest and best fans from gay community. Of course, I am nobody here and now no one knows and cares about me, but at least I will suck some of the positive energy they are spreading around. You really should get a gay friend if you don't have one already. They are the best and they will never give up on you.

All these times I have been to UK, I never had a chance to explore the city like a true tourist. There is so much to be seen. National Museum is amazing with all those masterpieces in one place. You could easily spend a whole day wandering around and absorb the greatness from the walls. It looked almost identically as in our world. By going even further, it looks stranger to me. It doesn't even feel like afterlife. Seems so the same as it was before I crossed over.

The time to go the theatre finally approached. We ate some delicious vegetarian food at the restaurant that was part of this complex. As I already mentioned, we had seats in the first row. The theatre itself was very small but very cozy and accommodating. The stage was at the same level as the seats.

I read in the newspaper during the breakfast some synopsis about the show:

...This play deals with two sets of friends and the mixed feelings they all have for one another. It is a story of love, marriage and upset as we are introduced to Stinky and Jake, plus Hedda and Delila. With Jake feelings directed towards Hedda, Stinky plans to marry Delila, but all of this threatens to be undone as terrible advice and some hidden secrets make themselves known....

✼ ✼ ✼

I was intrigued by it even more. When Mandy told me it's a comedy, I knew I have to see it.

The play started and instantly I became amazed how close I was to the stage. The door opened and a half-naked posture moved right in from of me. I thought, God thank you for this half-naked man in front of me. To make this work, just take other 100 people off this place and dim the lights even further. Yeah right, in my dreams. Nothing like this happened of course. Lights came up and a 50-something Adonis with hairy chest started to oil himself. God, kill me now. Oops, I am dead already. This must be hell then, you can watch but you can't touch. Shit! For the whole play I was observing the class act of all actors. There were only four of them, but the play was amazingly witty, cleverly directed and very funny. I felt like at home sitting and watching the action happen. It seemed that the play ended too quickly. I always felt good things don't last long and in this case it came true as well.

Mandy had her face wide with a huge smile for the whole show. She surely enjoyed the play very much as well. Afterwards we had a chance to meet the cast. This was supposed to be a custom here at this theatre. That gave me even bigger thrills.

- Oh Mandy, Thank you honey for this night. I loved it so much. I wanted to jump on the stage and consume the body of this adorable, super sexy, funny and talented hunk. I haven't had so much fun in a long time.

* * *

- I don't think I need to say anything else. You saw me darling. I was in a trance watching it the whole time. I enjoyed it as much as you did. So great to have a good time for a change. Let's go back to the hotel, we have a flight to catch tomorrow.

CHAPTER THIRTEEN
RIP on trip ?

It was very tough to wake up the next day after whole night of first-class entertainment. Plays like this should be showed on television. Maybe people would appreciate true talents more, instead of imbeciles with huge butts and no brains. OK. Stop with the lectures. If you're reading this you already must have the same taste as I, otherwise you would enjoy something less subtle like "Doll's Shithouse Confidential"[wink], you know what I mean, right.

After quick breakfast we headed to the airport. Mandy received a call that there is a problem with our tickets. We wanted to sort the problems out as soon as possible, so the fast ride was the only solution. When we arrived, Mandy left me with the bags and went straight to the information desk. I grabbed all our stuff, Max wasn't complaining, and moved slowly after her. When I came, I was informed that we have a choice to make.

❊ ❊ ❊

- Joan, our plane is cancelled. But there are two places left on the charter plane directly to the Rabac. We could be there in a few hours.

- Ladies, you do not want that kind of excitement – lady from the help desk explained.
- Why not?
- This plane is really low class. Let me show you. You have been traveling first class so far. The plane you are about to embark is here, economy is here and first class is here.

- OMG, Joan. This is deja vu or else…. I saw the movie on the plane and something exactly like this was in it. This can't be true. No, No, No.
- Mandy relax. What the fuck did you see? Final Destination shit?
- No, it was a comedy about the psychiatrist searching for happiness.
- It doesn't sound bad. Did he survive the flight?
- I think so.
- Had he found the happiness?
- Not during this flight he hadn't.
- Woman, get your stuff sorted. We're taking the tickets. This can't be worse than transparent elevator.
- Jenna, we're taking the tickets.
- Ok ladies, I have warned you. Here are your boarding passes. Gate 89 right wing. Enjoy your flight.

After saying that, Jenna, our ticket master, went to the back office laughing. Let's hope it's not going to be a ride to hell and beyond.

※ ※ ※

For sure it was not first-class experience with dining, cocoons, driverless cars and shit like that. We had to walk to our special airplane. When we arrived at gate 89 our jawbones went almost to the floor.

- Honey, do you see what I see?
- Yes darling. Are you sure we want to flight this thing?

Max looked at me and started to laugh quietly. Mandy noticed that and said,

- Joan, is Max laughing?
- Oh Mary look at that.
- What, where …?

That gave me few seconds to whisper to my beloved pup.

- SHUT the fuck up you little asshole. Do not laugh in front of her.

Max started to laugh harder and went bezerk. He flipped out and started to act like one crazy dog would.

- Joan, there is something wrong with your dog. Is he alright?
- Yes, he is. He surely doesn't want to meet any European bitches. Isn't he?

- OK Joan, there is no return. We have to go on this plane. Two hours and we will be on the beach drinking cocktails.

- Good, let's do this.

With all my scary thoughts on my mind, I grabbed Max, my bags and went in the plane's direction. By all means, I am not afraid of creepy surroundings as many times in my life I visited hideous pubs and clubs to perform (buck is a buck, right). This plane was something totally opposite of the one we have flown from Hollywood-end. First of all it was small and smelly. One corridor with two seats on both sides times thirteen rows equal fifty-two possible casualties. Fanta "fucking" stic, isn't it?

We took our places. Creepy steward with a cigarette in his mouth started to explain safety rules. The belt he was using was really outdated and obviously not capable of helping when needed. Max looked at me with his grumpy face. I briefly whispered to him to calm down and it's only two hour long flight. When the steward dropped the safety belt and went to the pilot cockpit, I really started to be worried. Airline was called Air Maqumba and I doubt it would be allowed to fly in the "real" world.

Our places were located on the wing. I wasn't surprised as the seats were not numbered and people already had taken the best spots on the plane. Believe me, on this flying bomb you wouldn't like to be seated on the wing.

※ ※ ※

We moved forward, plane started to squeak when speed increased. When we were driving with the take-off speed, I was imagining the plane breaking into half. Once we started to lift I have noticed our wings began to move more harmonically, up and down, than I ever saw on the planes before. Max pressed his head to my back trying to hide from this disastrous situation and was heavily shaking. I gave my bud a kiss on the head and started to calm him down a bit. When we reached the cruising altitude, I could finally relax. It was not a comfortable situation I must say. It was stable enough to take a deep breath.

- Mandy, slap me in the face when I ever decide to go on something like this again.

She gave me no response. Her body was paralyzed, she was looking at the ceiling. I knocked her on the shoulder gently and finally got response I was waiting for.

- What the fuuuuuck was that?
- Was what? Me punching you or the start?
- Are you playing with me Joan. Of course, the start. I have never experienced something like that in my whole life. Believe me, I will slap you if you ever decide to go on plane like this again.

Maybe it was 50 minutes or so we have been into the flight and started to fly over the Mediterranean Sea. Sky we saw through the dirty windows began to get more navy blue. It didn't look good. OK. I really, really didn't want to experience this especially on this plane.

Whole machine started to shake, thunderstorm sounds became more identifiable. Shit, we wanted peace and quiet for a week and now we have free shock treatment. Flying God knows what airline it is.

Flashes of light were crossing over to the cabin. Other people on the plane were very calm, talking to each other, occasionally jumping on the seats because of the turbulences. I think our triangle was the only one who was afraid of flying this piece of undiscovered aviation technology. I closed my eyes and waited with patience to finally land on solid ground. We were shaken a few more times before our pilot decided to lower the altitude of the plane and started to prepare for the landing. Clouds in light colors started to appear. When I approached the window with my face, I noticed beautiful turquoise sea. We are finally there. Mary send me your love through the airwaves.

CHAPTER FOURTEEN
Weird on a Wire

It's been 2 days since the meeting at the agency, and we were eagerly awaiting any kind of information about the possible job offer for Monique. In the morning as usual I went to the kitchen, fixed myself cup of coffee and went to the terrace to absorb some energy from the sun. Inside I felt a disturbance in the life-force. I hope girls are alright on the trip and nothing wrong happened to them.

I closed my eyes and took a few deep breaths, put legs on the chair in front of me. It was really a lovely feeling. When I started to stretch my body, I overheard the phone ringing from the corridor. I jumped right on my feet and ran to take it.

- Hello, this is Mary speaking.
- Hi Mary, it's Monique. I think I got it. On a trial basis, but got it.
- Awesome. Very good job, Mon. I have asked Ksav

to come tonight, please you do come too, so we could talk some more.
 - OK Mary, I will be at 6 p.m. Is that fine?
 - Perfect. See you at six sweetie.

Good news brought me a lot of positive energy to plan the day. I know that Mon was planned to trace and follow Farthashians, but I thought it would be a good idea to help the cause. After breakfast I decided to go and have a walk on Rodeo Road in hope to check out the famous shops, cafeterias and gyms.

I finished my cup of coffee, ate some sandwiches, dressed up, prepared sport bag with all necessities and headed for the city.

It has been a lovely day. Sun was shining and the temperature was warm and very nice to the skin. There was a slight wind coming from the ocean. Thanks to that, we had some fresh air instead of constant car exhausts. After I've packed everything that was needed I took a car (electric car, happy?) and went to the gym. Of course I never expected to meet Sin there, and I did not. I have spent an hour doing Pilates and some yoga to loosen up the stress that was accompanying me during all these days. After the class I went to freshen up a bit, took shower gel and wanted to wash down all my sweat. When closing the door of my locker I heard,

 - Hi there. How are you?

I closed the locker and couldn't believe who I saw. It

was Sin. She must have finished some private training session as I haven't seen her anywhere around the club.

- Oh hello, Good Afternoon. I am OK. How are you?
- I am bored. I am Sin by the way.
- Oh my God, where are my manners. My name is Mary.
- Nice to meet you Mary. Are you new here?
- Yes. It's my first time here. I am very stressed lately and needed loosen up a bit so I took Pilates and yoga class. What do you like most here at this club, any particular exercises?

- I have a private instructor. How about nice cup of tea afterwards? Do ...

Sin's face got a grimace on and she looked at me with a strange look and said.

- What are you looking at bitch, now move!

I was totally shocked. Once cute and nice girl and suddenly bitch from hell? I have moved away from her, took a quick shower and afterwards headed for the exit. While leaving I noticed Sin making a scene at the reception. I took a moment and waited in the car to see what will happen next. Few moments later, black SUV with darkened windows arrived. I heard the honk twice and saw Sin leaving the club. She slammed the door with a huge amount of power. For a moment I thought, why these are not rotating doors, that would be funny to see. Once she entered the car, it moved very fast.

※ ※ ※

Without hesitation I followed the car, but I wasn't quick enough to see where they were going. Few intersections later I lost them. That was it, my first meeting with the celebrity everyone talks about. In short – crazy and weird.

I let go the shopping and cruising Rodeo Road. On my way home I grabbed some food and drinks for the tonight's meeting with the girls.

CHAPTER FIFTEEN
Mon got a job!

6 p.m. was approaching very fast. As an appreciation for the girls, I have booked us a section at the fancy store in the Lost Angels. Not retail store, comedy store, sometimes I am babbling without rhyme and reasons. We need to laugh some more for a change.

Girls arrived slightly after six. As the show was scheduled for 7 p.m., we decided to eat something in the city. We had the limo waiting for us in front of my house exactly at 6:20 p.m.

- Mon, Ksav, you will never believe who I met earlier today. I wanted to wander around the city shops, cafeterias and gym to take all this stress off my mind. At first I went to the LaRura gym, took a Pilates class and then did some yoga for relaxation. When I was about to hit the shower, a nice sweet girl talked to me. It was Sin Farthashian.

※ ※ ※

Mon asked with interest:

- No way, how was she, tell us everything.

Ksav was listening to the conversation with very intrigued face expression, like she was expecting something she already knew.

- Well, as I said, after the class I was about to hit the shower and that woman we know from TV, billboards, commercials appeared in front of my face. She was friendly and asked me to go with her for a tea after the gym, when suddenly something happened. I do not know what it was, a grimace on the face appeared, she grabbed her head with hands. After few seconds she looked at me and said: What the fuck am I staring at? I was totally blown away by this sudden change. She left the locker room, and I went to have a quick shower.

- And, something else? That was it?
- No honey. I am not the type of gal, who easily surrenders. When leaving the club's premises I have noticed Sin giving bad time at the reception. Decided to spend some time in the car to see what happens next.

- What happened next? Oh my God, cut to the chase woman.
- Mon darling, relax. It's not a horror story. Relax and listen.

- While waiting in the car, I have heard two honks from the approaching black SUV. After few moments

Sin went off the club, jumped into the SUV. I was not able to keep up with the Farthashian and her crazy driver. Few intersections later, they were gone.

- Well, now that was something weird. Ksav, you haven't said anything. Is everything OK babe?
- Monique, Mary, I have noticed similar behavior at her home. We have been doing some laundry the other day and have seen something like this. I never knew nor suspected what could be the reason for being this way. She has two best friends that are always around her – Pamela and Jacob – and her behavior seems to be influenced by them. They are very friendly people from what I have noticed.

- Are they also her managers?
- I don't know that Mon, I am only cleaning there. I was never interested in the more deep secrets of the Farthashians. To be honest, I didn't care what they are up to. I wanted to do my job best possible and get the hell out of there.

-OK, I understand. You know Ksav, I got the job on a trial basis. My first day is on the day after tomorrow.
- Great, I will be there too. Mary, stop thinking too much. Everything will be just fine. Where are you taking us anyway?

- Sorry ladies, my brain froze for a second. We're going to laugh out loud at the "Comedy Store". I have heard that Richard, John, Gilda and Chris are performing tonight. It should be very memorable and pleasant evening.

- That is awesome, right Ksav?
- Yes Monique, I loved John and Chris in the past. They are very funny people.

We arrived to the show with the perfect timing. We grabbed ourselves the drinks and the show began.

Gilda started to entertain the audience with her physical comedy sketch. She was later joined by Chris who also was known for similar skills. They played mother and fat son. They were sensational. You wouldn't need any drinks to enjoy that type of comedy. If you have some like in our case, it's an explosive combination. You can hardly breath.

After them, Richard and John took the stage with their naughty and sometimes cruel jokes. Everything was perfectly mixed with the newcomers who graced the stage for the first time that night. We all had a blast. With happy thoughts straight after the performance we went to the restaurant for a supper. Ksav agreed to listen more carefully to what is going on in Farthashians house. Monique's first day at work was coming up very soon.

CHAPTER SIXTEEN
Is that a beach?

I was thankful so much for this disastrous flight to be finally over. Once we touched down the airport in Rabac, I haven't been so grateful in my life. The airport was not state of the art, just one lane that could only accept smaller planes, just like ours.

When I stepped out of the plane I kissed the ground. OK, I know, I know it would suit the Pope better, but was so happy to finally get off this flying relict.

I stood up and took a wide look on the surroundings. It was amazing, almost to die for (something like this almost happened for the second time). The scenery was like from a movie. Beautiful turquoise sea and gorgeous mountain like landscape with small bays here and there. Max was pretty happy too. He jumped right out and went to take a piss on the nearest tree. He turned around and winked at me. It must have felt good

❊ ❊ ❊

Finally, Mandy took her ass off the plane. Looking like on a crack, she barely was able to walk.

- Joan darling, help me out please. I can barely walk. My ass hurts, I cannot move my neck. This was disastrous.

- Mandy, open your fucking eyes. We're out already. Snap out of it. You wanted to fly, you have experienced hell, now you are on the ground. Forget it. We will walk back home. Is that what you wanted to hear? Are you happy with that?

We have had enough of that. We got our stuff and went straight to the resort. It was placed near beautiful bay on the hill with most beautiful view on the island Cres. I was about to enter the area of beautiful five star resort when I heard Mandy.

- Joan. It's not the one. I overheard you wanted to be a tourist and so you will be. I have booked us a room in tourist village. Not to worry darling, everything will be included and we will have view on this beautiful scenery.

Mandy took a charge this time as well, she's a bossy bitch I never thought she was. I knew she could talk you to death, but this trip is giving me a different view of her. The reception as well as the "village" was not in one building. It was beautifully spread around on the coast of the city surrounded by the pine trees. I loved the smell and the place. Once we checked in we were given a key to our room with the information about the resort.

Our building was located approximately 30 meters from the sea. It wasn't the first-class experience but it was clean and accommodating. Honestly I expected something even worse, but hey, I was surprised in a good way. Our room had a terrace placed with the view on the sea and the island Cres. As we had been located on the last floor, we had the perfect view of the surrounding area. I liked it so far.

Mandy started to be more energetic. She must have really wanted to get of this plane. We left the baggage in our room and went for the short tour of the city. Croats are really friendly people. Everybody is smiling at you, you are giving them the best of you as well. That really is relaxing atmosphere. Building we were staying at was just in front of the long sidewalk. We took the stairs from the hill and went in the direction of the city center.

As it's been early September, temperatures were not that high as during the summertime (July–August). The humidity was very high and when we got to the resort it was hard to breathe for a short period of time. We went further along the coast. Many hotels and spa's were located on our right side on our left beautiful sea. It was totally transparent and you could see the bottom of the sea without any problems.

I was looking around with concern, where are the beaches? Such beautiful surroundings deserve gorgeous looking and wide sandy beaches. Yeah right, I could look for hundred more miles and I wouldn't find any. Mandy explained me that the Croatia is known also for its rocky beaches and no sand. OK, No sand, no waves.... I think I can live with that as long we will have some peace and quiet to talk about things.

While walking on the sidewalk we have noticed a train with the tourists approaching. Max started to bark. I asked him,

- Do you want to get on this buddy?

Max started to run in circles.

- OK, OK. Mandy, let's hop on this train.
- Fine Joan, as long we're on the ground.

We jumped into the train. It was a quick ride, but it gave us a tour of the best city spots. Max was very happy. He wondered around on my knees looking from side to side in search for his own kind. Once we stopped I had to drink something stronger to loosen up a little bit. In the harbor I noticed several drink bars open. I took a seat near the water and ordered some "Sex on the Beach". OK, Rocky beach.

- Mandy, what's next? We still have over a week. Do you have any plans? Why am I asking that. I am sure you have, you are awesome planner.

- Actually no. I want this trip to be a surprise to me and to you from now on. Whatever you want to do I am open for it. We can take banana ride, and we can go and visit Venice. Choose what you want.

- Venice, you mean Italy? If yes, I am definitely up for it. As for the banana ride I will think about it. I think I am too old for that kind of fun.

- Tomorrow we have to call the girls and check out what is going on.
- Good idea. It can give us more free time as some of the things we may plan could already be prepared or even solved by them.

- OK. That's tomorrow. Let's enjoy our drinks now. Look at this place. Small paradise, I would never visit it if it wasn't for you. Thanks Mandy. Cheers!

CHAPTER SEVENTEEN
First day

I was very stressed before my first day at Farthashians house. I was asked to come at 10 a.m. sharp, casually dressed to meet Sin in person and to get more details on what to expect from this job. I already knew that they wanted me to take care of the PR stuff and small things that might come up. I wasn't worried about job itself. I was afraid of the Sin herself. Knowing that she acted like a weirdo during her unplanned meeting with Mary, I expected even more shit coming from her, not in the public space.

It's been 9 a.m. already. I checked everything once again: the outfit, makeup, bag and its contents, everything seemed to be on its place. I said to myself.

- You are ready for this bitch!

With that said, I have closed the door of my apartment and went downstairs to the car. I got the address from my bag, typed it to the navigation equipment and started to drive. I turned on the radio and finally some relaxing music started to play that made me feel so good. It was a concert of very talented and very, very young artist Jaclyn Evanco. The song that started to play melted my heart. The title was "Pure Imagination". I almost wanted to close my eyes, but the technology did not allow me to do that while driving just yet. Maybe in the future something like this will be available for everyone.

When driving through the city I started to think about the possible outcomes of this first meeting. I promised myself to keep an open mind and not focus only on Sin's behavior but rather explore the site's deeper secrets. Maybe I was influenced by this music. I have no idea. Suddenly I became a better person. Hush, hush, Mon what are you thinking? You have to get that talentless bimbo.

I finally arrived at the destination. The house was huge, looked like a small palace with the gorgeous driveway, thousands of flowers and trees around it. I told to myself. Such a fantastic place should be occupied by somebody who truly deserves it, not by someone who is famous for being famous. That doesn't even make sense.

It was exactly 10 a.m. I have knocked the door. After a moment a butler opened it and greeted.

- Good Morning Ms. Szymolinsky. Mrs. Farthashian

is expecting you along with her agents in the salon. Please come with me.

While walking through corridor I noticed beautiful paintings and furniture. What can I say – that bitch has a good taste. When I arrived to the salon, Sin and with the managers that interviewed me were sitting behind the desks.

- Hello there, I am Sin Farthashian. On my left is Pamela and on my right is Jacob. You already know them, they interviewed you and knowing that it is very hard to get through them. Congrats to you. From now on you're on a trial basis acting as my personal assistant.

- It's supposes to be a PR-related job.
- What did you just say? Complaining already. You just came and started acting like someone too good for being my personal assistant.

Sin started to yell at me and became furious practically without any reason. I noticed Pam and Jacob were disturbed by it. Suddenly, Sin grabbed her head with a hand and whizzed from pain, I suppose. She calmed down a bit, sat down on the chair and started once again.

She described me my duties. Basically I became her personal bitch. No wonder the earlier one left after the month. Having someone like Sin on daily basis may only be horrendous affliction, nothing else.

❈ ❈ ❈

- Monique, Mark the butler will show you around the house. I will see you in an hour. We have to discuss tomorrow's schedule.

- Thank you Mrs. Farthashian, I am very sorry you got my question this way. I am very happy to be here and to help you with everything you would want me to.

- Now that's better, Monique. Now go. I need some time to myself. See you in an hour.

Mark looked at me with "The Look" and said.

- Come along Ms. Szymolinsky.
- Mark, Can I call you Mark?
- Yes Ms. Szymolinsky, you can.
- Please call me Mon. Mark, is she always that way? Does she act like a weirdo with everyone in here?
- Unfortunately yes, especially with her servants, maids and cleaning ladies.
- How long have you been working for her?
- Ten years this July. Is this an interview?
- No Mark, don't get me wrong. Just want to know what I have stepped into, that's it.
- You are acting like the previous assistant. I don't even know what happened to that poor thing, she quit after a month, did you know that?
- Oh yes, I was told that it happened. Maybe she had enough of this, I wasn't told the reason of her departure.

During our tour I briefly noticed Ksav cleaning one of the rooms. She nodded when she saw me. This got

Mark thinking.

- Do you know her?
- No, I do not. I simply like people, always smile when I see someone. Is that bad?
- Of course not. Sorry Mon.

I didn't want to blow my cover and kept our friendship as a secret at least for a while. First I need to know people better before I trust them.

- Mon this is your room.
- My room? I have my own apartment. No need for me to stay in my room 24/7.
- This is just in case. Nobody will keep you here by force. Unfortunately, Sin is having very vivid personal life and staying up late will be quite frequent.

Our tour of the mansion continued. We went through huge home cinema room, very spacious dining space with the beautiful wooden table in the center. I have noticed heart-shaped stairs to the first floor and to the basement. I wasn't taken anywhere else. After a moment Mark walked me to my room and asked to wait here.

The room that was supposed to be mine was really nice. There was a huge desk with computer, telephone and bunch of binders, books, notes and newspapers on it. Seemed normal. Turned on the computer and started to browse the notes that were placed nearby. Everything looked like a busy environment. Bunch of meeting notes, information about the photo shoots, TV show tapings.

On the bottom shelf of the draw I noticed a spiral notebook tightly closed with some sort of a special mechanism. I took it to my hand and tried to peek inside through the angles. Just noticed few words, beware, butler ... It was impossible to get more of it. I put it into my bag as it seemed to be kind of interesting to pass.

On other side of the room was a bed with nice looking painting hanging just right above it. On the left was an entrance to the private bathroom. For a moment I thought - Shit, I can save on some bills and move here. Of course that was out of the question as my job was related to something more valuable than being a private bitch to someone famous for being nobody.

It's been quiet outside so I opened the door of my room and sneaked up to take my own private escapade around the house. I went in the direction where I saw Ksav to have a word with her. I moved quickly to the other room. Ksav was dusting the books on the shelves and was a bit surprised when she saw me standing behind her.

- Hey Ksav, what's up girl?

- Nothing much, Sin is preparing something for tomorrow and we have so much work I can barely move now and it's still more to do.

- Sin acted like a psycho when I disagreed with

something she said. Freaks me out a bit, and the butler told me that there is a room for me. There was never any mention about me staying here overnight. Was this the same with the previous assistant? Have you heard anything about her while she was here? I have to know why she quit. Can we get her name at least to find her and talk to?

- I have no idea. I can browse through the documents while cleaning her office. But she is not much of the person who takes notes. Her managers are doing everything for her. She just plays dumb girl on her TV show, they tell her everything and she does just that.

- While browsing the room I have found a notebook but it's locked somehow. Still have no idea what may be inside but tonight we will try to open it with Mary. Maybe you could come? It's still early in the morning maybe you will be able to get some info while cleaning. We need to get some information soon. Girls are on vacation but they are counting on us.

- Good then, we will meet tonight at Mary's place. I hear someone coming. Hide there.

Ksav showed me a closet. I knew it's awkward but didn't want anyone to see me here talking to Ksav. I jumped in squeezed between the clothes. They smelled so good. I heard the voices coming from outside.

- What are you doing here? I heard the voices coming from this direction.

- I am cleaning here Mrs Farthashian. I have been reading book titles out loud. Maybe you overheard that.
- I know what I heard. Are you trying to tell me I was wrong. Who the hell are you to judge me.
- I am so sorry Mrs. Farthashian. I didn't want to offend you in any way.

- Good, because if you would I would kick your sorry ass out of here right this second. Now go back to work. I am not paying you to read books.

Sin forced closed the door and left the room.

I opened the closet door and looked at Ksav with worried look.

- I am so sorry Ksav. I better go now. I don't want me to cause you any problems. We will speak in the evening. Keep your eyes open.

I hugged her goodbye and left to my room. I wanted to be as quiet as possible, grabbed the handle and opened the room's door. Sin was sitting behind the desk. Fuuuuuuuck.... So this is it, I thought.

- Where the hell were you? We have so many things to do.
- I went to find you. It's been almost an hour.
- I am having two things tomorrow I need you to help me with. First, taping of another episode of my show and afterwards I am hosting a party. Mark already knows what to prepare, you just come along in case I

need anything. Plus you will learn something. Oh my God…My head … aaaaa … what is going on with me? Who are you dear?

- I am your new assistant, Monique. Is everything alright with you Mrs. Farthashian?
- I am fine, just my head it hurts so much.
- Mark, Mark, please help. Something is wrong with Mrs. Farthashian.

I heard someone running into our direction. It was Pamela who came as first. She started to scream.
- Jacob, Jacob, come on over here. Something is wrong with Sin.

After a moment Mark, Pamela and Jacob appeared. They took Sin and went downstairs. Pamela turned around and said:

- Monique, You have rest of the day free. See you tomorrow at 7 a.m. sharp. Taping starts at 8 a.m. Do not be late.

I took my bag and left the mansion. While walking after behind them I have overheard quick conversation between them. It shouldn't happen. What is going on with her? That sounded even creepier than Sin's behavior. I said bye to all and left the building. Jumped into my car and started to drive home. This whole episode got me thinking. There is something deeper going on in this fucked-up place.

CHAPTER EIGHTEEN
What is this about?

I really started to worry about the Monique's first day at work so I decided to call her wondering if she pick up. I dialed the number connecting showed up on the screen and to my surprise and happiness Mon picked up.

- Hey girl, what is going on? Is everything OK? How's is your day?
- Relax Mary. It's cool. I have things to tell you. I have met with Ksav at the mansion talked to her briefly and almost got caught. Discovered a notebook but it's sort of locked. Can we come tonight? We will check it out and maybe Ksav will have some news for us.
- Of course, of course. Come anytime you want. I will wait for both of you.
- I can't talk much right now as I am driving home. See you tonight.

Driving home? It's 1 p.m. What happened in the middle of the day that she could go home. That surprised me a lot. But hey there is an explanation for everything. She said to be cool and not to worry. I'll try to do just that.

I sat in front of computer and started searching for Sin's previous assistant. I didn't know her name but that was not the point now. I browsed the pictures from the events and started to analyze them. There were thousands of photographs, TV show stills, premieres, special events, etc.... I could probably spend weeks viewing them all. What I have noticed wasn't any spectacular. Same facial expressions, gorgeous dresses, beautiful people around. I am not saying she's not pretty. She has something for sure. I do not what it is, but she is sucking in all those viewers in front of TV sets every week. On few pictures I have noticed the same woman. Photos were taken three months ago. She always was staying in the background, well that's for sure. Her look was very casual, nothing special, neither pretty, nor ugly. For sure, our Monique has breathtaking looks, she could easily out stage the Sin. To be honest I had no idea whether it was her assistant on those pictures or not.

I really wanted to call the girls straight away and ask for the advice but I decided to wait until I get some more information from Ksav and Mon. I had few hours left before girls' arrival so I went to the deli to get some food for tonight. I knew Ksav will be tired after whole day at work. I am sure she will not have much time as she has six kids to take care of.

※ ※ ※

Traffic these days is pretty awful. Shopping took me few hours and with not so much time to spare, I prepared delicious dinner made of "sandwiches". Come on, I am not a kitchen expert.

Mon came on time but there was something wrong with Ksav's arrival. So far she was always punctual.

- Monique, how was your day?
- Nothing special to be honest. I have been staying at the mansion only for 2 hours or so. I have talked to Ksav, found some diary/notebook that is locked and I couldn't read. Sin got crazy and after a while become nice and sweet person. Then she was taken away by her managers and butler to calm down. They took her to the basement. No biggie as you can see, it was very normal, I say NORMAL day.

After a brief moment we started to laugh. How normal is that. Then I have heard the knock on the door. It was Ksav and her three youngest children.

- Hi Mary … Oh Mon, hi babe. Sorry girls, I couldn't leave my kids alone. The other three have sleep over at friends. I didn't have time to find babysitter at the short notice.

- Sweetheart, no problem. You do not have to explain anything. Please do come in. Hello kids, my name is Mary. I made some sandwiches. You must be hungry after day at school. Would you like some?

※ ※ ※

They looked at their mother, she nodded it's alright. I took Ksav's kids and we went to the salon. I asked them to sit on the arm chairs and wait for a moment until I get back with the food and drinks. I went to the kitchen and grabbed freshly squeezed juice and the plate with sandwiches. When I arrived at the salon, kids were chatting quietly among themselves.

- I am back. Here's the food and drinks. To make this more enjoyable I have something very special for you. On this disc I have most beautiful story ever played. It's called "Alice in Wonderland". It's like a theatre in your head. I hope you will enjoy it as much as I when I had been a child. I pushed play and went back to the girls.

When I entered the dinner room they were already there discussing notebook that was found by Monique earlier today.

- Ksav, this is so tightly closed. Do you have any idea how to open it without destroying it?
- It's really well sealed, but look here, there is a spiral part that could be removed. Oh Mary, all OK with the kids?
- Everything is great. I see the notebook. Can we open it?
- We think so. There is a spiral side of it, maybe we could cut it through without destroying the contents.
- I think I have something that might just do the trick. I used this to cut the wires.

I have brought the chisel and we started to carefully

cut the spiral part of the notebook. We managed to cut through it and were able to force open the rest of the book without destroying the pages.

- What is this about?
- It looks like a diary to me. Each page has date, time and place. I think we will be able to learn more about Sin's whereabouts.
- Look at that. She has also noted the strange behavior experienced by us. She wrote,

July 4th
Sin was acting like out of her mind in the morning, she was yelling at everyone couldn't agree on anything. Suddenly she changed to someone totally different. She was kind and polite like I've never seen her before.

We have browsed throughout the pages further,

July 15th
Another meltdown, this time it was worse. Sin collapsed and was taken to her private room in the lower part of the mansion...

- Mon, does it sound familiar?
- You took it out of my mouth. Ksav dear, have you noticed something like this?
- I haven't. Maybe something like it happened in the past. I've never been analyzing her behavior so much until today.
- Until today? What do you mean?
- Mon, when you left I heard some voices coming

from the basement. I heard male voices discussing something. I moved quickly back as they came out. For sure, there is something going on. You will have more opportunities to get inside and see what it is. I can keep your backs in case something happens.

- We have a plan for tomorrow.
- Very good then. There will be a party tomorrow night after filming of the final episode of the season. It should be easier to get to the basement and see what's there. Sin asked several cleaning ladies to be present during that time. So I volunteered.

- Perfect! Let's go to the kids and spend some time with them.

CHAPTER NINETEEN
Paradise city

Mandy and I for sure enjoyed Sex on the Beach too much yesterday. It was way too good to cut at first approach, so there was a second, third, fourth and final fifth. We were so wasted from top to bottom, we barely got back to our room. We might have even forgotten about Max as I don't recall him coming back with us.

- Max, Max … are you there? No response.

Shit, it doesn't sound good. He's not here. Fuck, how could I lose him on our first day here. I dressed as quick as possible, put on some shoes and went for the door. I grabbed the handle, opened the door and he was sitting right in front of me.

- Where the fuck did you go?
- Me? You have been inhaling alcohol like a pro last night. You probably don't even remember what happened. For sure something was itching you from

below the waist, as after fourth drink you decided to go to continue the night of drunken revealing. How about that?
- Do you know what happened?
- Shit, I am not your mommy. Besides you locked the leash. So you went, I stayed. Thanks for fantastic vacation so far. Shit, if that wasn't for that super cute Croatian babe I would still sit there.

I overheard Mandy waking up.

- Joan, you here?
- Yes babe I am over here, look who's here. Max decided to come home.

Max looked at me.

- Are you fucking kidding me? I decided to come back home. You are a pussy sometimes.

While walking towards Mandy, he turned his head around showed me a tongue and made a face.
- Come here my little boy. You are so cute, oh yes you are. Aunt Mandy will hug and kiss you.
Max ran to Mandy, jumped on the bed and started to cuddle with her like he used to with me. Jealousy, sweet jealousy. I haven't felt that in quite some time.

- I think we have a breakfast coming up. Shouldn't you be ready Mandy? Move your cute butt and let's go. Max can come with us. They have a patio.

* * *

Mandy went to the bathroom, took a quick shower and was ready like new in a matter of minutes. I was starving.

- Come along guys…

We went out. The restaurant was located in the separate building. We had to walk there for about few minutes. With fresh air coming from the sea and the pine trees around, the mixture would give a boost to anyone, even us drunks.

Once we arrived, I got a bit frustrated. What the fuck is this. Forty people in the queue to get inside? What is this place, is this a restaurant or fast-food joint. I was a little bit pissed but once we got inside everything started to look much better. I have managed to book us a table on the patio. I have also noticed that this place is "buffet" style joint. With that known I have asked Mandy to get something for herself and I was ready to keep an eye on our seats.

- Ok darling, when is your turn, please bring me some sausages, boiled carrots and some rice. Oh and some sparkling water if you may.
- Honey and what else would you like, caviar and wine too?
- Don't be a bitch. You brought me here to eat not to watch you stuff your faces with food, right? Jeez sometimes I think you are even more fucked up that I thought. Shit, I am out of here …
- Max, I am so sorry. I am a bitch. Happy now. Sorry

pal, I'll bring you whatever you want. We are a team and we should act like one. Can you forgive me?
- Mhmmm. Give me a kiss. Mhmmm, that's better. Let's leave all behind us –forgiven and forgotten. Mandy is coming.

- Mandy, finally. What took you so long?
- You will not believe how many people are inside. You have to literally fight for food.
- So I will fight. See ya in a few minutes.

It was not as bad as Mandy described. Of course there were a lot of people, but the place was huge and there were so many varieties of food. I took a plate put some delicious-looking veggies, eggs, some salad with the dressing. I have not forgotten about Max. Got him what he wished for: couple of sausages of different kind and some cooked veggies. Suddenly, a very handsome guy approached me, hugged and then kissed me like I never was kissed before in my life.

- Hello gorgeous, feeling rested after last night?

He sounded American. He was tall with dark hair and brown eyes, handsome looking kind of guy. He had an awesome smile and I must say he wasn't a bad kisser either.

- Good morning ... and you are?
- Joan, don't say you're not remembering me. It's John. We met last night at the club. We have been dancing...

- Just dancing, right?
- Well not only dancing, we drank a lot too. Maybe that's why you do not remember much from last night.
- So you know Mandy too?
- How could I forget? You were the funniest and the most entertaining women in the club.
- Well John it's nice to see you again, I think. We have a table outside, come and join us for the breakfast.
- Thanks, see you in a bit. I have an eye on this tasty-looking salad.

I took my plates and went back to our table. When Max saw me he started to frisk. I think he wanted those sausages very badly.

- Here you go buddy. This plate is for you. Mandy do you know any John?
- John, John, John ... Doesn't ring a bell.
- How about now? He's coming in our direction.
- Ringidingiding ... that John... Now I remember darling.

John's walk was really firm and catwalk like. He had a great presence and everyone looked at him with envy, especially men.

- Looking flawless Mandy. How are you? Oh ... Hello little fella, nice to meet you too.

Max looked at John with his well-known "look" and continued to eat the food I have brought him. He wasn't struck by his "mojo" as we were.

※ ※ ※

- So John, I presume you are American right?
- Sure, I am.
- Is this your first time here. We have just arrived yesterday. If you could help us with the sightseeing we would really appreciate that. Wouldn't we Mandy?
- Of course, of course, we would Joan.
- It's my first time here. I have arrived a week ago. For sure last night was not the best to introduce myself properly. I am John Catalina owner of the Celebrity Network. You know the TV channel. One of the most popular ones in Hollywood-end. What such a wonderful ladies like yourselves do for a living?

- We're cheap whores who suck cocks for drinks, right Mandy?

Mandy started to choke, threw up everything that she had in her mouth.

- Of course, she's kidding John. We're not cheap. How could you Joan.

Mandy and myself started to laugh. John finally figured it out that we were messing with him.
- OK ladies, you are hot, funny and smart. Love it! I'll be happy to show you around as this place has so many surprises to offer. You didn't say what you do for a living.

- We're journalists. We love to travel and we write articles about our journeys.

- Sounds boring.
- Yeah right, like "Meet the Farthashians" is more exciting.
- Joan, you watch it? This is our most popular primetime show.
- I have seen few episodes and I was beyond excited, way beyond.
- Well then, we have a #1 fan here. Maybe I will be able to arrange a meeting with your idol.
- Oh really. I cannot wait.

I looked at Mandy and said with my lips
- Is he fucking kidding me or what?
- I gotta run now. Can we meet at midday right over there?

John showed us a bench in front of the beach with a lovely view.
- Sure can. See you in a few hours then.

Who would have thought. Celebrity Network executive same place, same time as us. We can squeeze all the info we can about Sin and her whereabouts. That sounds like a plan.

CHAPTER TWENTY
Paradise city - part 2

Jeez! I am so stuffed after this breakfast. I think after such load of alcohol last night, I should at least have a slight hangover, but no, I feel great. I ate like a horse, and so did Mandy. We are now so buzzed off after the coffee they served us. Phew! We're definitely ready for some action with all that power in us.

We had our meeting with John scheduled at 12 noon. We still had some time. OK, it was not much, an hour or so. Mandy, Max, and myself decided to have a short walk to the harbor to check if there were any private excursions we could possibly have. I know it sounds boring, but you can't always do extraordinary things. Sometimes you need to chill out and relax.

I noticed a small travel agency located nearby and without hesitation went inside their office.

- Hello! Do you speak English?

- Of course! How can I help you ma'am?
- First, don't call me ma'am. I am not 81-fucking-year-old broad. Do you see any wrinkle anywhere in here? I don't think so ... and yes you can help me.
- OK. So what can I do for you?
- We would like to rent a boat, preferably big enough to hold three adults and a dog.
- A dog?
- Yes, this dog to be precise. Is there any problem with that?
- No, no problem, Boat 13, in the harbor. What time do you want to start your trip?
- 12:30 p.m. will be just fine.

I paid the lady in advance and left the office. She apparently was not expecting something like this. Well, I don't care as long as we can have what we want. While walking, I overheard someone speaking English. I turned around and noticed a cute gay couple.

- Hi boys! If you don't mind me asking, has anything been going on in this town?
- Hi, depending what you mean by "anything". You can do sightseeing, dance, drink, do some spa, eat good food, and swim in the cleanest sea in Europe.
- That is exactly what I meant. You mind showing us some nice places tonight. Haven't seen many English speaking crowds around.
- We're Polish.
- No shit, at least I understand what you're saying. Why did you talk in English? Can't you speak Polish?
- *Ich spreche auch Deutsch.*

- What did you just say? You better not insult me pretty boy.
- Who cares what language I speak. You understand me, I understand you. What's the big deal?
- Not much. Let's just start from the beginning, then. My name is Joan, this is Mandy and my dog Max.
- Well, that's better. I am Ralph and this is my partner Michael.
- Nice to meet you guys. Cinema bar 8 p.m. tonight?
- Cool! See you then.

What the fuck was I thinking, picking strange gay guys on the street of Croatia? Whatever, at least we will have some fun tonight. You can never go wrong with cute gays, can't you?

When we got back to the room, it was almost time to go and meet John. We put some tanning lotion on, gorgeous looking hats, some light clothes, and went to the meeting place. He may be surprised with our excursion.

Walk from the hill didn't take us long maybe 5 minutes. John was already waiting for us. He looked handsome. Being in his 40s, he happened to look even more attractive than the most of the 20–30-year-olds. He had that look and smile that could easily shake knees of any woman. Yes, even you my dear.

- Hi John. Ready for the adventure?
- What do you mean by that Joan?
- We have a surprise for you, okay for us. We have booked a boat, so we could sail around the coast and

view some of these fabulous landscapes. Have you tried that before?
- Actually no. It's a very good idea. Let's do it.
- We have to be at 12:30 p.m. at the harbor, Boat number 13.
- 13?
- Don't say you're superstitious.
- Of course not.

He must've been lying, because suddenly his facial expression changed from "I can do everything" to "holly shit, we're gonna drown." Honestly I didn't give a damn what he was feeling. He's an executive; he will deal with it one way or another.

Our boat was ready and the captain waved to use once we approached him. It was more a yacht than a boat. It looked somewhat sporty but with enough room to comfortably seat, drink, eat, and enjoy the views. That's what we, OK I, needed. I really dreamed of having some time off. Being a workaholic all my life, I finally started to appreciate the relaxation and chill out.

Once we entered the deck, the captain started to prepare for departure. He unattached the rope from the dock and closed the entrance. Couple of minutes later, we started to move. I thought John must have been happy to see the sea to be very calm without any wave. Enough with him for a while. I know opposite attracts but at that time the best thing around was the landscape of the Rabac's coast. On one side, we could observe people frying their bodies on rocky beaches, our lovely sidewalk with multitude of pine trees and hotel. On the other, colorful sea ranging from light blue to turquoise and ending with navy blue. We happened to have a very good weather; there was almost no wind, sun was shining with occasional clouds now and then, and we had the boat for ourselves for the next 4 hours.

We took our places on the front deck and started to undress with Mandy. Max took a place in the shadow and took a little nap. I know his naps very well. One part of his brain never slept. He was practically conscious all the time and at this time he better be. I need him for support. He may be one little pervert but he was here before me. Information taken from John may be valuable for us at the later stage of our "plan."

- Oh Lord, I missed that. I told you Joan, it will be a pleasurable experience.
- So true Mandy, so true. John, do you enjoy this country. As an executive you must have been to many fabulous places, haven't you?
- Actually no. I do not like to spend extra cash on something extraordinary. Croatia is beautiful — no celebrities, weather will not surprise you, and best of all you will be able to afford practically everything without any major leaks from your bank account.
- Really, I would suspect someone like you would love to be surrounded by celebrities, beautiful actresses, and rich people, but you are a penny pincher. No offense.
- Just because I exploit them on TV doesn't mean I like to spend my free time with them.

※ ※ ※

Exploit them? WTF is he talking about? This word is too strong even for this conversation. I wondered what he meant by that. I knew network is getting a lot of money for these freakish shows, but people are willing to act dumb for the money, no exploitation intended.

- What do you mean by exploit them? It doesn't sound right.
- What I meant by that was they will do everything for the money and fame, no matter how long it stays. People are pretty much stupid and will do practically everything for the money.
- Is that so? What about Farthashians?
- Sin is very special to us.
- Special? She's special for sure. I have no idea why she's so famous. She's plain dumb.

Though his explanation was quite convincing, I didn't like the word. That got me suspicious even more.
- One time I was watching "Spoiled and Dumb Kids of Beverly Halls." Are they "exploited" too?
- Hahaha... No Joan, they are just plain dumb and if people want to watch them on TV while giving us bunch of money, it's a win-win situation here.
- Okaaaay...
- Something wrong?
- No, No, No ... everything is good. Who's up for some swimming? Mandy, Max, move your cute asses up and let's go.
- Joan do I have to? My chocolate body needs some warmth. I don't want to go inside this cold water. John you're going?

- Actually Mandy, water is not cold. After a long summer of high temperatures, it's kind of warm. Come on babe, let's do some swimming.
- OK honey, if you insist.

Mandy jumped right from the sun bed, took off all her clothes, and jump right into the water. With her cute naked butt, she sure gathered some audience. Captain stopped the boat, looked around, and said under his nose *"ludi amerikanci"* and started to laugh. I thought for a moment "no one knows us here" and took all my clothes off and made a splash bomb near Mandy. I noticed Max picked his ass up and went to the edge of the boat, looked down, and moved back. John looked at him and said.

- What little buddy, fancy some swimming?

Max looked at him and said ...
- After YOU!!!!!!!

John was surprised as hell, Max was moving in his direction and it happened. John flipped the birdie and turned overboard with all his clothes on. I, on the other hand, felt something moving around my legs. I freaked out a little bit, and started to swim in the direction of the boat. Suddenly, before my eyes a dolphin appeared. Dolphin here, I thought. That got be calmed down. I used to be close to those smart and gorgeous-looking animals in the past. He started to come closer when my moves became more peaceful. He even allowed me to touch himself or herself. Maybe it was a girl; I have no idea. That really made my day. We had some more fun in the water and decided to call it quits. We got on the boat and relaxed for the next 2 hours. Captain took us on the trip near the coast of the island we saw from our hotel windows.

Normally I am a pushy broad who gets what she wants, but in John's case I have already heard what I wanted. Hopefully our spies in the Hollywood-end will do a better job. Our trip ended and we went to our hotel room to get ready for lunch, and evening with my new gays pals.

CHAPTER TWENTY-ONE
T.r.o.u.b.l.e

I couldn't sleep all night before the show taping and the party at Sin's mansion. I knew that I am professional, but I had a gut feeling that something will happen. Maybe it was just a bad thinking followed by an awkward first day, who knows. But this thought didn't want to leave me. I knew I had to look sophisticated during the party, but had no idea how to work it out in between recordings of the show. Last afternoon, I called Kenny and asked him for advice. He helped me once, maybe this time he will think of something extraordinary. After a short chat over the phone, we set up a very early meeting. I drove to him at 6 a.m. to get advice and some clothes that I desperately needed. Considering that I couldn't sleep the whole night, I really was eager to see his magic done on me.

It didn't take me long to get to his place. Even so it was very early in the morning, he was glammed up. That was not the point really, as I wouldn't mind to see him barefaced. As this was his day off the show, he was not wearing lady clothes. He looked like handsome man, with bright smile and full of positive energy. He did the magic on my face and with my hair. Everything looked fierce, I thought so. I tried on some dresses, and they looked good on me but not perfect as I wanted to.

- Kenny, I would like to outstage Sin this evening, to see how she reacts. Do you have something with "WOW factor"?
- Honey, I think it's going to be very hard to do it. She has much more money than we do. But, once I was doing a private show for the very famous "star," I will not mention her name, and received as a token of appreciation a very special dress.
- OMG! please, please, please, show it.

Kenny went to his wardrobe and returned with the big box. Once he opened it, I was mesmerized by its content. It was a beautiful, red scarlet strapless gown with a large bow at the back. I wanted to immediately try it on. I dreamed this to be a perfect fit. Few moments later, it came true. It looked flawless on my body. Of course, I never intended to wear it now. I wanted to make a splash entrance for tonight's party; so I packed it back to the box and took it myself to the car. I kissed and hugged Kenny for such an amazing dress. I promised, of course, to return it undamaged. I didn't want to be late, so put on the gas when road allowed me. I came to the mansion few minutes before 8 a.m. In front of the house, two big cars were parked. I noticed TV equipment was being brought inside for the installation.

It seemed quite normal. I knew that, as I have been working for TV station for 5 years now. I sneaked inside and started to search for anyone I knew. After a moment, I noticed Pamela and Jacob talking to Sin. Maybe it was some sort of preparation, but they went downstairs. I knew I had to get there to see what's happening there, but this was not the right time for any exploration. I thought that during tonight's party it will be much easier to infiltrate the surroundings, when people are loud and having fun in the main salon.

Then, someone at the door rang. Mark did not hear it, so I decided to open it. On the other side, there was the whole Farthashian family—funky mother, father with slightly altered face, and Sin's sisters. For a moment, I thought, what the fuck was their father thinking? He looks so hideous like hell. Let's hope his nose will not break off his face. The rest of the family was kind of normal. OK, their behavior was slightly altered, probably because of the fame and fortune they got. I wonder how normal they were, before the show even happened. I greeted them, explained who I am, and let them inside. For them, it was a day like no other. Never thought of it what they done as an acting. Being themselves and doing nothing extraordinary didn't seem to me like something useful for the humanity. I also never got it, why people are so fascinated with mediocre family and their boring, yes very boring, lives. You may be watching shows like this in your free time. I wish you could tell me, why are you doing this? Is your life so boring that you need the view of someone else's lame stories to appreciate yours more? Maybe it's just that.

But if it's true, we can come to the conclusion that tens of millions of people are either depressed or not enjoying their lives to the fullest, and they need cheap substitution in the form of Fathashians.

The whole family went to the main salon to browse the screenplays for the episode that was about to start being recorded. Screenplays, I wondered, in place I would expect much better stories and more interesting action. But that's not me for to decide this. I am merely an assistant here. Sin was walking in my direction.

- Finally, you are here. Observe and learn how big bucks are made of. I need you to make some calls, for catering, live band, and bakery. Today we are filming the final episode of the season. Tonight's party will become a part of it. It must look perfect. Now, just leave. Mark will give you more details. I need time for myself to focus on a play

Holly molly, what for? It's hardly a theater play or a movie. Anyways, I went in search of Mark to get the details of the companies I had to contact with and make sure everything will be flawless tonight. We do not want to piss off our Big ass ... or do we?

- Oh Mark, finally I have found you. Sin wants me to take care of the bakery, live band, and the catering. I guess they were all ordered by now, weren't they?

- Yes, they were. She probably wants you to confirm it. Here are the details. Make sure they come earlier.

Party along with the filming starts at 7 p.m. They must by here at least an hour earlier. And for you, wear something more glamorous for the tonight.

- I will, no problem.

Having everything prepared, I already knew everybody will have eyes on me instead of Sin. I sincerely hoped she will have her anxiety "attack" in front of everybody. I took all the phone numbers and began to call the services. They all knew everything and were planning to come to the mansion at the agreed time. It was not hard to achieve. It took me maybe 30 minutes or so. I went back to the salon, when the show began to be filmed. It seemed so badly acted and the problems they were trying to picture for me happened to be so dull and egocentric. I tried to look like overwhelmed and very interested in everything that took place during the filming. I had to keep the appearances, I wanted to get their trust and interest, and I could only achieve it by acting my way up. I noticed that even small fascination from someone they barely knew meant a lot for them. Were they so self-absorbed and bumptious? I sat there and watched the action for the whole time. The filming was moving from room to room, kitchen, and outside terrace. The episode was revolving around Sin's possible pregnancy. She recently got involved with a mediocre rapper, Lamey East. He was much worse than Farthasians, no talent but huge ego. That's the worst possible match in the traits of character. As you may have already experienced in your own lives, many talentless celebrities have that two features in common, haven't they? No need to reply, I already know the answer.

Family took a short break from filming. They approached me and started to ask questions.

- Hi there. So how did you like the segment of the show?

For a moment I thought, should I tell them the truth or lie? I am an honest person, but the stakes were pretty high and needed to cover my personal feeling for this unbelievably average piece of junk.

- I loved it. You are so real and fabulous.

The smiles on their faces started to appear. Having said that already moved me closer to them and they started looking at me from a different angle. As there was a 2-hour recess between the filming, they asked me to come with them for a short brunch. We took the limo and went to the nearby restaurant. Sin did not come with us; she wasn't in the mood for it. Like being in the mood was her specialty. When we came to the destination, another show started. These "kids" started to behave like they were a hub of the universe. Demanding something to be delivered right this second, I couldn't stand all these little bastards. They seemed so spoiled rotten assholes. They were practically known only because of the show. They did not achieve anything in their pathetic little lives, but they all demanded star treatment all the time. Good for me, this brunch didn't take long and within an hour we got back home.

The second and final taping started. I decided to wonder around the house a bit more as I had less eyes on me. I got downstairs where Sin was taken few times during my stay in here. Unfortunately, I couldn't enter the room. Doors were very well closed. Barely got back up without a notice. Barely ... and Mark saw me coming up the stairs. I increased my speed and went back to the filming location and started to look busy. I opened the laptop and began to make notes. Mark didn't proceed in my direction. For this time I got away with excessive lecturing and questions about my wandering around the house. Now I knew that there must be something very important.

During the short break, I was approached by Sin.

- You are not coming to the party looking like this, are you?
- Of course, not.
- Good then. Wear something simple, but classy. I have ordered more help to come. Be sure everything is taken care of.
- I will, not to worry.
- We will see about that. Now be gone. You can wait until the party in your room. I will call you when you're needed.

I went to the car to get my dress. Took everything I needed to do the makeup and moved to my room to prepare. Put on some relaxing music and went to the bathroom to get a nice aroma bath. For a moment, I thought I fell asleep and yes I have. Not for long, thank God. I rushed from the bathtub, wiped out myself, and started to prepare my hair. As they were already very well cut, styling them and putting in right direction would not take me long and would be pretty easy to achieve. Makeup on the other hand would take a little bit longer. I didn't want to look like overdone whore with tons of makeup on the face. I had to follow the golden rule of makeup. Less is better. I had mineral makeup powder, mascara, and lipstick. That should do the trick and be perfectly enough for evening party especially combining it with the lovely dress I got from Kenny.

Time of the party finally started to approach. I put on my red dress and total package looked really good. I looked from the windows and noticed people arriving, many people to be precise. It looked like red-carpet arrival, without the carpet.

I overheard that the show and party already started. I closed the door of my room and went downstairs to the main salon. On my way I met Ksav. She took her hands and covered her mouth from the surprise. She was so happy to see me looking like this.

- Monique, you look like a star. Go get them. I will be around if anything is needed.
- I am afraid Sin will freak out. Too bad, this show is not broadcast live. That would break a viewing record for sure.

- Hahaha, It might. Go get them.

I started to go downstairs and the roar began to be more noticeable. I was a bit shaky, who wouldn't. I was nobody for them. I finally reached the salon. First person who noticed me was Mark the butler. He approached me quietly and said:

- Looking hot Ms. Szymolinsky.

I really didn't have to wait any longer as the people nearby started to approach me. I never thought this dress would pull people like a magnet. I was so thrilled to see so many new faces. People were very kind and wanted to get to know me better now. Compliments about my looks were pouring like rain. Once I was talking to some lady, I got approached by Pamela and Jacob. As they haven't recognized me from behind, they were shocked when I turned around.

- I see you're wearing Vera's creation. Very nice, but don't you think it's too star-like? You are not a star. You should pray that Sin will not see you now. It's doubtful as she's "the one" to watch on this party. Try not to be the center of attention.

Well, that's very good to hear. I took my cute butt outside of the salon in search for Ksav. As everybody is having fun, I should have more time to explore the basement. I needed a support to get through the door.

- Oh Ksav, Ksav.

- What is it Mon? Something's wrong?
- I think we can explore the basement now. Everybody is so absorbed with the party, and we have a chance to see what is the place Sin was taken to after the attack.
- I think we're in luck. At the time you left the house yesterday, they took Sin downstairs. I went after them and noticed special pad hidden in the wall.
- Have you noticed the code they were using?
- I think so.
- Come on, it's too obvious and too easy to be true. I am sure there must be some catch to this.
- I don't know. Let's go and see.

We looked around with anticipation, and no one was there. We quietly went downstairs. There was a door; alright I have seen that before. It was on the right-hand side of the staircase. I expected a numeric pad where you enter combination of numbers. Instead of that there was a screen where you had to draw a special sign. It was dark there, and we didn't want to turn any lights on to be not discovered. Ksav started to draw the sight on the display. We got error message.

- Ksav, I think the lock like this must also have an alarm. Do you really remember how the sign looked like when they entered it?
- I am really stressed right now. Maybe we shouldn't do it.
- We have to. It's the only chance we're gonna get. Try one more time.
- I remember they started from the top right, moved

down a bit then to the left, then down, all the way to the left and then to the right.

- Let's try it. I think we have three chances.

Ksav draw the symbol. ERROR! displayed again. We had only one more chance.

- I know, I know it now.

She tried one more time but ended the bottom line at the edge of the display. We heard the lock open and were able to enter the room. What we saw wasn't a typical room we expected. Once we closed the door and turned on the lights, sophisticated laboratory appeared before our eyes.

- What the hell is this Mon?
- Seems and looks like a laboratory to me.

Whole room was equipped with state-of-the-art computers. They were located all over the room. In the center there was a main console with huge armchair. I am not a scientist or tech guru, so it was really hard for me to comprehend what would be the use of this. Was this a monitoring chamber of everything that was going on in the house? Suddenly, we heard screams and voices coming from outside of the room. There was an extra place that you could go to from the lab. With no other choice, we hid ourselves from the upcoming company.

The door opened.

- It should work longer. Why the hell she is changing so quickly? The procedure should be effective for at least one day. This predictive programming is not working. You said it's going to be permanent at some point.

Women voice answered.

- This is an ongoing process. Few more times and it should click. Then we will be settled for good. Put her on the armchair and get the diodes on her skull quickly. I have prepared special program. This bitch will rock this party hard and the episode will get the best ratings. Now do this fucking shit. Did you hear that?

- I didn't hear anything. OK then. Turn this on. We can't waste any more time; people will get suspect. Good that the Lamey turned the way we wanted. He's a perfect idiot, hahaha.

- Oh yes he is, and this stunt during concert with this crippled person. Amazing publicity! Bad PR gave us extra millions of dollars. My only concern is with the baby. If she's pregnant, we have to think of something.

- Let's leave the kid alone. In 10 years we will be rich enough to ditch those assholes and retire for good.

- Shit, something is wrong. Did you check on Angela? We have to get rid of her somehow. We can't keep her forever.

※ ※ ※

My phone started to ring. It was Mary. I picked it up.

- Mary we're in the basement of the Farthashians mansion ....

Pamela overheard something, entered the room, and noticed me. Thank God, Ksav managed to hide behind the sofa. Pam slapped my face. My phone dropped down. She picked it up and took off the battery.

- You little bitch. I knew there is something weird about you. Another spying whore came to the town. Mark I think we have a problem. Pick her up and take her to Angela.

Ksav silently got off the room and slowly started to go through the laboratory to the exit. She managed to get out, but the door slapped hard and Pamela heard that.

- You better tell me now. Has anybody else been here with you?
- No! It was just me. I was looking for the bathroom and ended up here.
- Don't lie to me. These doors are always locked. You couldn't get in here just by accident.
- They were open, I am telling the truth.
- It doesn't matter. You know too much.
- Mark, take her away. I'll finish with Sin and bring her back to the party.

Mark grabbed my hand and brought to the end of the room. There was a switch. Once pushed, the wall moved and another room appeared. Inside there was a young lady. I was pushed inside and the doors were locked.

- Who are you? I asked.
- I am Angela. Sin's assistant. How about you?
- Me too. I just got the job, and I think I have found your notes in your room.
- Let's hope you're not the only one who knows about it.
- We will be out soon.
- I wouldn't be so sure. Have you seen the lab? They are planning something.

That got me worried. What if they use this machinery on us? Ksav, Mary, Joan ... I need you ....

CHAPTER TWENTY-TWO
Somebody's somebody

I barely managed to get out the room. Ran upstairs, wanted to look normal. Went to the maids room and took my bag. Without any hesitation I went to the car and drove away as soon as I could. Honestly I started to worry about my life. After hearing these crazy people I truly hoped they didn't know about me and Mon didn't spill it.

I drove to Mary as I needed to tell her all about it. She probably wouldn't believe me as I hardly believe myself. Mind programming. How is this even possible? I drove to Mary for good forty minutes. It was late when I got there. I parked in front of the house and ran into the door. I started to push the bell many times. I was so stressed I really wasn't thinking what was I doing. I simply had to tell someone. I had to tell Mary. Bell didn't bring Mary down so I started to hit the door with my fists.

※ ※ ※

- Mary, Mary. Open up. Please it's very important.

After few moments doors opened and Mary appeared. I was in tears, shocked, scared and shaking.

- Oh my God Ksav, what is going on honey.
- Everything is wrong. Mon was kidnapped and may be dead by now,
- What are you talking about. How is this possible, what happened.

- Remember the diary we read the other night? We have found a room that actually is a laboratory. Sin and her husband are programmed to be the they way they are. They are using some sort of advanced techniques. I barely escaped but Monique is still inside. We have to help her.

- What are you talking about? How is this possible?
- They are programming people for they own use. They tell them what to do, how to behave and everything in between. They are behind the scenes but taking all the cash.

- We have to let girls know. We won't be able to do it on our own. You can't get back there. It's not safe anymore for you or your children. Where are your kids now?
- At home, because of the tonight extra hours I have asked babysitter to come.
- Come inside and go call her. I am sure nothing will happen until tomorrow. I will prepare hot cup of cocoa.

Tomorrow we will take your kids and move to my home. We can't risk anything happens to them.
 - Very good idea. Thanks Mary!

CHAPTER TWENTY-THREE
Say Bye Bye ... NOW

I haven't had so much fun in such a short period of time ever in my life. This vacation is giving me so much joy you wouldn't believe. I can't ever recall in detail what happened last night. All I remember is laugh, laugh, dancing, kissing, great music, and my new Polish buddies, John and Mandy. Max?

- Max, are you here? I said quietly.

For a moment, I thought I lost him again. Shit, this son of a bitch would not forgive me second time for sure. I looked around the room, and Mandy was sleeping like dead, but I haven't seen Max anywhere in the room. I stood up and started to walk around the room and checked all the places he might hide. What the fuck is going on with me? Seriously, for the second time I ran to the terrace. What a relief! He was there and not alone to be honest. He found his bitch after all. Max and his "chosen one" were lying side by side with their faces directed at each other. They look so cute together. I didn't want to wake them up; so I got back to my bed to chill out for few more minutes. Suddenly, my phone started to buzz. Text message arrived.

SOS. Please call as soon as possible, Mary

I instantly took my phone and started to dial Mary's number. No response. ERROR showed up on the screen and I could not connect to any number from now on. It's not usual to me but I started to freak out.

- Mandy wake up, NOW. It's urgent. I got strange message from Mary. I am unable to call her back. Try to do it with your phone.

- What? What? What do you mean you can't call her? Let me try.

Mandy did the same thing, but no response.
- Holy cow! Let's try the landline.
She dialed the number from the landline phone. Still not working.

- Mandy, something must have happened. We have to get back, NOW!
- Honey, I wish it would be so easy. We have to rebook the tickets.

For a second I thought. JOHN. Maybe he could help us. I couldn't tell him what we're up to. A little lie would not hurt him. On the other hand, I have what I wished for. Action, full calendar remember? Who would ever expect that relaxing situations I like the most now and would throw this planning as far as possible.

I knew we had to take our asses and fly to Hollywood-end as fast as possible. This may be my new life for me but what if something will happen to the girls? I would feel terrible if anything happens to my best friends in afterlife. Better yet, is there something like dead for the death? I do not want to think of it.

- Max wake up, we're going for a walk. Take your babe with you. Mandy, I am going to see John, maybe he can help.

We went outside as soon as possible. John was living in the nearby building. It was a short walk. Max stayed outside to chill out for the last time probably, as we're leaving no matter what. The building John stayed at was in a bit better condition than ours was.

Corridors had more lights and everything seemed better quality. I remembered well his room number. It was 213. I went to the second floor straight away. I got more stressed with every stair and on having finally arrived, I knocked a few times on his door.

- Joan? What are you doing here so early? Something happened?
- We have to leave home as soon as possible. Our friend is in trouble.
- Can I help?

- I was hoping for that. We have tickets booked for next week, but we need to go now.
- Relax, everything will be OK. Come here.

John hugged me very tight and tried to calm me down off the emotions, which clearly were out in the open.

- I have an idea. A plane should come for me next week, but will be happy to help you out. Let's meet after breakfast at the airport.
- Really? That's fantastic. How can I ever repay you?
- You will, one way or another, someday.

I kissed John for goodbye. I thought, such a great guy he is—classy, intelligent, handsome, and rich. I didn't want to lose any more time. We have to pack and fly back home.

-Max, where are you?

Suddenly from the nearest bushes Max walked off with his "BITCH." OK, OK, I am not going to say anything. He wanted it, now he got it, good for him.

- We have to go now, we're flying back home in a few hours. Give your girlfriend a cuddle and move your cute ass.

When we got back to the hotel room, Mandy was already packing. She didn't know that I managed to find a solution for flying back home. She was a mess. Last night was truly crazy and wild. I will skip the story because you would totally change the perception of who I become here. Although it would be something you'd never done yourselves. Maybe someday soon I will tell you more about it. I know you'd like that.

- Mandy, good news. We can fly home! John will help us. We have to be ready to go to the airport somewhere after breakfast.
- Don't worry, I have everything under control.

Well, it did not look like having "under control" to me. Her wig was somewhere misplaced on the head. As we were exhausted after the party, she still had her makeup on, slightly altered. She looked so funny. As the alcohol did not have any effect on me here (no day after syndrome), I asked Mandy to go to the bathroom and take a hot relaxing bath and prepare herself for a flight. She wasn't complaining and went straight away. I packed everything quite fast to all empty bags. At this time I was not thinking what's mine, what's Mandy's, just wanted to have all in the bags. Max wasn't happy about early departure, but he understood the importance of this situation and tried to behave without sulks. I admired his behavior as I haven't seen a "man" who could quit on nice pussy so fast.

Mandy finished her bath and "beauty enhancements." To my surprise she looked flawless. I couldn't tell she had a "blast" last night, you wouldn't too.

- Are we ready?

- Mandy, wow! You look amazing. How could you do it so fast? You have to teach me few things babe.
- Nothing much, usual stuff. Are we going to the airport now?
- We still have some time for breakfast. I think you would appreciate some coffee, wouldn't you?
- You took it out of my mouth. Let's go.

We were the first to arrive for breakfast, so it was no queue for us. We ate something easy to digest, drank few cups of coffee, and head back to the hotel to get our bags, and Max of course. We checked out and asked a taxi to pick us up. When it arrived, I remembered that we have no gifts. I knew we had a situation but had to buy something for the girls and especially for Ksav's kids. I asked the driver to stop for a moment near the promenade and jumped off the car to get something.

There was a toy stand with cute handmade dolls for girls and remote control cars for the boys. I also bought collection of honey varieties with nuts and figs inside, for the girls. We will need some sweets after we clean this mess. Once I bought everything, we could go to the airport. When we left the taxi, I noticed John waiting for us.

- Ready girls and Max for an adventure?
- We just want to fly home. No adventure needed.

We came through the small airport and went in the planes' direction. I haven't been focusing on the planes much. John started to talk about his aircraft.

※ ※ ※

- How do you like my plane?

Hell no, are you fucking kidding me? I didn't know who to slap, probably myself and would get another slap from Mandy. On the runway, there was an AirMaqmba plane awaiting departure. Mandy looked at me with the look and started to prepare her hands to hit me hard.

- John, AirMaqmba is your airline perhaps?
- Air what?

The plane started to move and right behind it a small business jet was standing. I took a deep breath and relaxed. No bitch slapping for me today.

- I own this small business jet. I hope it's alright.
- Of course, it is. Forget I said anything.

Steward took our bags and put into the bag section of the plane. We entered with caution. Phew! At least our ride home will be without any problems. Plane was really nice, nothing like the "jet" we have flown from London for sure. Six comfortable seats were enough for me at least to start this journey back home. I really didn't want any more surprises. I didn't know what to expect when we arrive. It was a mystery to us what the hell has happened.

The plane started to take off. John told me that we have to stop in London for a moment to get fuel for the further fly home. Mandy and Max already fell asleep cuddling to each other. I, on the other hand, started to look outside of the window.

CHAPTER TWENTY-FOUR
Joan to the rescue

Our flight was very pleasant and without any major problems. Some slight bumps happened, but I knew nothing serious would happen to us. It was very late when we arrived at LAXXX airport. I thanked John for our rescue and safe flight home. Mandy was relaxed after uninterrupted sleep. She was even surprised to be home so quickly. Well, it was not quick, maybe for her as she was sleeping for the whole time. Once we get off the airport with our luggage, we had to find taxi as soon as possible. I tried to call Mary one more time, but without success. I have noticed one cab was released by the passenger who just came. We ran in the cab's direction and a second before me a young guy opened the door and went inside. I said to myself, Oh no, you little son of a bitch, this fucking cab is mine. I managed to open the door, as I was a bit pissed and tired after this crazy day.

- Didn't you see I was running in to the cab?

- So what? I got here first grandma.
- Oh no, you didn't, you little motherfucker. Move your ass or else ….
- Or what granny? Your dog will bite me? Ohhhh, I am so fucking scared. Move bitch!
- Oh no! I will slap your fucking face so hard your plastic surgeon will not even recognize you.

I grabbed him and pulled him off the cab. I used all my power. Suddenly once he was out, I got a flashback. I knew this asshole. Yes, it was a spoiled and rich dumb fuck from the show. With that in my mind, I didn't even want to apologize and ask him to free this cab for us.

Mandy asked the driver to pack our bags to the trunk and took a seat with the Max in the rear seats of the taxi. This spoiled asshole started to curse and threaten us. I showed him a middle finger and the car started to drive. I gave the driver Mary's address and tried to calm myself down. It didn't take us long to get to our destination. It was very late and the roads were almost empty. I jumped right of the cab, Max went after me, and Mandy took care of the bags and the driver. I went straight to the door. The moment I wanted to ring, the door opened. Mary noticed someone arrive at the house. When she saw us, she came straight to greet us.

- Joan, Mandy, I am so happy to see you girls. You too Max….
- What happened? We tried to call you but your phone was not responding. I got your message and did not know what to think.

- Come on, get inside.

I noticed Ksav standing in the corridor, very sad. One of her kids was standing right beside her. I ran in her direction to hug her. I opened my arms and we hugged so hard, she started to cry. I asked

- What's wrong honey? Where is Mon?
- Everything is wrong.
- Well? Where is Mon?
-That's something we do not know. She was caught at the Farthashian's mansion, long story.

I could not believe my ears. Once Mary and Ksav finished describing what happened during our few days of absence I could only say, WTF? I thought our world was fucked up, but this one is getting even creepier. We had to prepare something to get Mon back. She may be easily brainwashed by these freaks and then we're screwed for good. I knew we had to get back to the "House of freaks" to search for Monique, that's easy. What was not so obvious was how to get inside. Send another assistant for an interview? Come on, you must be out of your mind, it's out of question. We need someone unknown with four feet and hairy back to see what's and who's inside.

- Girls, I have a plan but I have to execute it by myself. I don't want you to be involved for safety reasons. I love you too much to risk anything happens to you. When time is right, I'll share all the information with you. Now please don't worry. Let's go to sleep, and tomorrow everything will be over.

- Why are you so sure about it? You're not going to ask John for help, aren't you?
- I will not, trust me.

I went to my room, and Max followed me like he knew what I had in store for him. I sat on my bed and took few deep breaths and lay down.

- Max, you do know what I want to do, don't you?
- I think I do. You can't go there, so you're sending your dog. How classy, shit.
- Don't be an asshole, you wanted action, wanted to help, now here's your chance.
- OK, OK. What do you want me to do?

Honestly, I had no idea. I was tired and my brain took off. I desperately needed some sleep.

- All I know now is that we have to drop you by the house and hope they will let you in.
- Mhmm, interesting idea.

The next day I woke up first, dressed up quickly, took Max, and left the house. I took the car and I have to think over the plan I drafted in my mind last night. Max would be ideal to see what is going on around the mansion. Maybe the other Farthashians have some heart to get cute dog under their roof at least for a little while. I spoke with Max and told him he must be let inside. As Ksav described, Mon was held in the basement room.

-Remember Max, hide somewhere downstairs and when the door is about to close, sneak in and see what's or who's inside.

- Easy to say babe, but how the hell am I going to get out of there?
- Act like a dog. They would never suspect you of spying.
- OK, I'll try.

We've been driving to the Farthashians house for quite awhile. Max was a bit stressed out, who wouldn't. I was thinking how to get inside myself. I will think of something. Now let's get him inside. All of a sudden, I got an idea. We should put a small camera on his collar so we could see what is going on with him while inside. I stopped the car and went to the office. I am sure they have something we could borrow for small investigation.

Once I got to the studios, I went straight to my office. I opened the computer and searched for the tech team in our intranet pages. I chose the cutest one and called him.

- Hello Bruce. It's Joan from "How you doin' with Joan and Mandy show." I need a favor. We're doing some investigation for our premiere episode and need something. A small camera we could attach to clothes and film undercover to be precise. It would be wonderful if we could watch the feed from the distance.

※ ※ ※

- Yes, that's exactly it. Can you bring it to my office, it's on 7th floor. You are a sweetheart. Thanks a bunch.

Bruce brought me a small camera that looked like a button, practically undiscoverable. He also installed a program on my smartphone, so I could see what's happening and record everything. I did not want to lose any more time and went back to Max.

- Hey babe, sorry for the stop. I have something for you. Look, a small camera. I will attach it to your collar. Thanks to that I will be able to trace all your moves and maybe help when you're in trouble.

- Trouble? Come on. You can't even be more supportive. Nothing bad is going to happen to me.
- I am sure there will be someone in the house. They were filming the final episode yesterday, so the whole family should still be there. They are your first chance to get inside. Walk around and try to find the entrance. I will be able to see all your moves and hear what's going on.

- OK, OK. Give this to me and let's go. We don't have much time.

We arrived near the house, not so closeby to be discovered. I was blown away. This shit looks better than all my houses and apartments together. I worked so hard for it. Why the hell someone gets it practically for nothing? Three sports cars were staying on the sidewalk, so it looked like Sin had guests. Having more people around would definitely help us. Bigger the crowd, more possibilities to explore, even for a dog. I opened the door of the car, let Max out, and asked him to do the job. I turned a phone to see if I get the signal correctly. Yep! It worked like butter. Max slowly moved in the direction of the house. This cam thingy was really great and made spying like something so accessible even for non-techs like myself. Max went straight to the terrace and pool. Smart buddy, obviously he wouldn't be able to get inside through the front door. Sneaky bastard. Max was naturally a cute-looking dog and even people like Farthashians should not resist his adorable act and look.

CHAPTER TWENTY-FIVE
Exposed

I always wanted some action in my afterlife and now I have it. This started to look like an episode of a detective series. Holly crap and I have a leading role. It was my time to solve this mystery once and for all. I went to the terrace hoping someone to be there at this time of day. It was quite early in the morning and I was not disappointed. Farthashians' sisters were sitting and drinking morning lattes. Believe me, I know how to be super cute. Just because I swear a lot, and respond like "a son of the bitch" to Joan does not mean I don't like her. Remember her? She always was making cruel jokes about her daughter and she loved her to the fullest. The same thing is with me and her, always was, and always will. I wonder how cute should I be, Cujo or Beethoven? Mhmm... Maybe I should mix both of them. What do you think? OK, that's settled. I approached them from the left. Being only cute probably would not cut, so I decided to act like a hurt dog. I started to limp and give strange voices. OK, they noticed me. Maybe I should cut on whining because they may think I have rabies and dumb Lamey would kill me, and I do not know what is next. I never thought if there is something like death for the dead.

- Oh Sin, Look ... a dog, something must have happened to him. He can barely walk.
- Shut up Loey. Who cares about this stupid mutt.
- Come on, show some empathy. Hello little buddy.

OK, Sin is a bitch, but this Loey seems to be quite alright. She took me on her knees and started to pet my head. It was soooo good.

- I will keep him and try to find his owner. But for now he stays, whether you like it or not, Sin.
- Whatever, keep him off away from me.

Phew! So I am in, almost. Sin went back to the house. I started to move more, so that Loey would let me off her knees. Opened my mouth and started to breath heavily. I wonder if she gets it. Holy cow! She is not that stupid as others. She took me home and gave a bowl of water. After I drank it, I went for an armchair, laid down, and pretended to sleep. She came by me and kissed my head, and head back for the terrace. I noticed a guy and a babe going into the basement's direction. I jumped off the armchair and went after them. Just like Joan said, I tried to get inside after them.

- Joan, I hope you can hear and see it loud and clear.

✻ ✻ ✻

I slowly moved downstairs. They entered the room and when doors were about to close, I jumped inside. They were so absorbed with the problem that they did not even look behind. I hid under the desk on the right side of the lab. I have never seen anything like it. They must be really into this shit a lot, to pull something like this. This must have cost them a fortune not to mention a knowledge. The couple started to argue.

- We can't keep them here forever, you know. We either convert them or brainwash and release to the world.
- I don't know boo. Check on what is going on there.

A guy went to the backroom to see as ordered, and got back after the minute with Mon.
She didn't look good.

- Hey you!

Mon looked at the woman.

- Yes, you spying bitch, I am talking to you. Feeling bad? Good! Put her back and bring some food and water for them. We do not want them dead ... for now.

Them? I thought only Mon was captured. The guy took Mon back to the room and left with commanding bitch off the lab. That made me thinking.

- Sorry Joan, I have to tell Mon about me talking. There is no other choice or explanation for me being here.

I went to the backroom and noticed Mon and other woman sitting on the armchairs with their hands tighten up with a rope. I approached her with caution. She noticed me and ....

- Jeez! Max what are you doing here?

I started to frisk and run to her. As I did not want to waste any more time, I started to chew the rope. Yuuuk, that tastes like a crap. After a moment, Mon's hands were freed. She picked me up and hugged.

- Mon, do not freak out, I said quietly.

At that time she froze, took me out front of her face and looked at me.
- Surprise!
- How? Why? What?
- Babe decide. I can talk so fucking what. We have to get the hell out of here.

Suddenly I heard noises coming from the door.

- Fast, release the hands of your friend. We have to prepare to run. I will go and see what is going on.

I went to the lab and noticed three people. The same couple I already saw earlier and another woman. She was put on the huge chair in the middle of the lab and they did something to her head. It was freaky as hell.

Her eyes started to pop up, and strange facial expressions appeared on her face. I moved back and gave girls a sign for escape.

Mon took a chair and approached the guy who would probably be hardest to fight. She slammed his head with it like it was the worst murderer. She used all her remaining power to do it. The guy grabbed both the girls and all fell on the floor. Mon and the other woman who was kidnapped managed to escape from the lab. I went after them to see if they safely reached outside of the house. I didn't want to leave with them for sure, whatever would happen next should be recorded for the others to see.

I got back to the living room and jumped on the armchair, waiting to see what happens next. I hope this camera is recording everything. For sure Joan and Wendy's premiere show would get a huge boost in rating when this shit is showed. The couple ran from the basement. The guy's head was bleeding and he had a huge bruise on his forehead.

- How these bitches got their hands loosen from the rope? It doesn't look good. They may go straight to police and we're fucked up.

- Oh, shut up. Stop acting like a baby. Who would ever believe them anyway? People messing with brains? Come on. Science fiction my asshole. We have to be careful and no more fucking assistants. Let's go back and fix Sin. When she's ready, we should take care of the rest of the family. When we have all under our control, we could rule!

- You shut up. It was not the plan.
- I want them to be my monkeys, and you will do what I want you to.

This shit was getting more "heat" than I previously thought. They went back to the laboratory. I followed them to the stairs. The doors opened and they kept them wide open. Sin was still sitting on the armchair unconscious. I have noticed the women injecting something on her neck. A moment later she woke up, was still dizzy, but managed to walk out of the lab.

- What happened to me?
- Nothing darling. You felt dizzy and fell unconscious for a while.
- My head! It's exploding ... aaaahhhhh.

She started to scream for a brief moment. Later, she got her head straight up and started to talk about today's tasks like nothing ever happened. This was weird even for me, and I have seen some fucked-up freaks in my both lives.

- Joan if you hear me, move your ass and get me out of here. Everything seems to be locked. Girls escaped, and sisters went somewhere I can't find them.

I started to walk around the house thinking that there must be something open to get out of here. I really liked the surroundings very much. Maybe not my style, as I need only a comfy bed, someone to cuddle with plus something to eat, but humans for sure would appreciate the luxury. I headed back to the living room hoping someone will show up.

I think, I have dosed off for a while. The sisters returned home with bags full of clothes and very happy indeed. Someone used the ringer on the door. I really hoped it to be Joan. One of the sisters went to open it. Yes my lord, it's her. I jumped right off the sofa and ran to her.

- Max darling, everything is OK. Thank you so much for taking care of my dog. I have no idea how he escaped and got lost.

- You live nearby.
- Yes. Not so far away. I moved recently from Europe. You have a lovely home here.
- You do not know who we are, do you?
- Should I?
- Of course, you should. What the fuck are you doing here and who the hell are you?
- Sin, don't be rude. It's ... You didn't tell me your name.
- It's Joan.
- It's Joan. She's the owner of the dog. She's living nearby.
- Oh! Whatever... I am leaving. We have few meetings about the upcoming TV talk show appearances.

- I don't want to interrupt you or anything. Thanks for taking care of my dog. Goodbye.

We went outside. Joan's car was standing on the sidewalk. Without hesitation we jumped inside and left for Mary's home.

- Did you see the action Joan?
- What action?
- Are you fucking kidding me?
- Yes, yes, I saw it. We have everything recorded. Good job Max!
- Well d'oh! ... I had enough of it. I need some time out. No more action for me at least for a little while.
- Hahaha, my hero who loves action is bored. No problem, I will take care of this from now on.

CHAPTER TWENTY-SIX
On air in 3-2-1

Ladies were already awaiting us, all of them to be exact. Our new friend Jackie, ex-assistant, was also there. Of course, Monique blurted out the "talking dog" secret to Mary and Mandy. Well, there is nothing we can do about it. I know what you're thinking. OK, we could bring them all back to Farthashians and erase this, but it's out of the question, got it? It's almost the end and you are more devious than I am.

When the emotions fell down, we all sat down in the living room to talk about our experiences. Fuck it sounds like a book club, hell no! It was nothing like it for sure. Mary brought her laptop and we started to watch the recording from the cam. Now that was heavy entertainment. All these could get them into so much trouble, but we should use this for our advantage, like a blackmail. You know maybe just the touch of love would help them, but I doubt we could give them that.

Everything was so clear and obvious from the recording. Even the footage was good quality and you could hear all the conversations, especially the one of Mark and Pamela arguing in the laboratory. Who would have ever thought they pulled up something like this, with all these people around them? I mean the family. All the sisters, they seemed different but their lifestyle adjusted to whatever they put to Sin's brain. Were they so money-centric assholes? Haven't they even noticed the changes?

The ex-assistant Jackie wanted to go straight to the police and report all of these, but with my power of persuasion I managed to keep her on our side. She was eager to take a part in our premiere episode. So it was decided all of this crap will be uncovered on live television. Who would ever thought that "How you doin' with Joan and Mandy" could become a blockbuster just after the first episode. And this is just a beginning of something extraordinary. We may have solved one case, but Hollywood-end still needs our help. These are going to be fabulous for the next 2 years, but we have to focus on the present and leave the future for the future.

Now it was time to prepare for the premiere. We had to arrange the first guests and from what we knew Sin was in a pursuit to advertise her season finale episode of "Meet the Farthashians." We should use that for our advantage. As Mandy was the only person she didn't know about, it became her job to take care of it.

※ ※ ※

- Mandy darling. Tomorrow is your big day. You have to arrange the meeting with Sin in regard to her appearance on our show. Her agents Pamela and Jacob would probably be the best to get in touch with.

- Yeah right like it's going to happen. We have assistants who do it for us. Monique?
- Hahaha, how funny you are Mandy. They probably already contacted the network. All we should do is to check everything out and confirm the taping date.

- Oh no honey, it's not gonna be taped. We will go live. Better, we should invite the whole family plus Sin's husband. He will do most of the job for us. Oh, and we need to have the entire row of disabled people.

We have been talking about silly things, but we or at least I do not know how our studio would look like? Come on, even better we should have some photo shoots and commercials running on the network. What is this place?

- Mandy we have to take more in our hands. Did you hear about any photo shoots or possible video commercials for our show? Does the management have any idea about promotion?

- I totally forgot about it with all this vacation disaster. We were supposed to do all that one week prior the first episode. It's tomorrow. So with all bad that happened to us, this "coincidence" will save our asses from being fired.

❈ ❈ ❈

How about that darling? You have managed to plan everything for our trip but forgot to take care of our show. Oyy, good for us I asked about it otherwise we, OK she, would be in a big trouble. I really wanted to have bigger control of the show starting with the studio and ending with the list of guests.

The next day Mandy and myself went to the office to check out the set of our show and to take a part in a photo shoot that miraculously appeared on our schedule. I went outside practically looking the way I woke up. OK, I didn't go in my pyjamas, but cut on special clothes and makeup. If it's photo shoot, I will let them take care of all these things. The photo studio we went to was interestingly designed and furnished. I wonder if this is a miniature version of the real studio for the show. Who knew? It had two desks on both sides and a huge sofa in between. On the back there was a blue screen probably for future editing. We were asked to go to the makeup and to dress up. On our way I noticed at least 30 different outfits for Mandy and me. Once we got to the makeup room, we were greeted by a lovely lady. Her name was Kate; she worked as a makeup artist for the last 13 years here at the network; so obviously she knew what to do with our faces. So good nowadays I do not need that much of the greasepaints and shit like that.

After some time, we looked like hot 40s. Most of the dresses that were selected for us maybe were not in style I would buy for myself, but have noticed one really excellent-looking, gorgeous red gown. There were two of them; so I asked Mandy to put it on. That would totally look great on the pictures. Two sexy broads working side by side, don't you think? She did as I requested and it was a match made in heaven, OK in Hollywood-end. We had so much fun-posing and making fun of one another.

After a while, we were asked to come by the monitor and see the results. Some of the pictures were hideous; you know I am very critical about my looks, always have been, and will be for years to come. But one of the photos really took my attention. The pose we took was really interesting. We were both sitting on the sofa, with legs crossed and the hands below our mouths and with curious looking grimace on the faces. I would only add a headline "We know How you doin'" ... plus the Hollywood-end sign arranged on the back and that's it. I asked the photographer to do the composition. It looked flawless; even Mandy was surprised how great idea this was. The photo shoot experience was really nice and we had a lot of fun. We kept the dresses on and left for my office. On our way Mandy asked the member of the tech staff about our studio. It happened to be already finished and prepared for the big premiere. That really was kind of strange. But I am not complaining, I am dead gorgeous and with lots of work on the horizon.

- Joan, let's go and sneak into our studio. I know the way.

Mandy led the way, as it was still new to me. My

third, maybe fourth time, being at the studios does not make any difference. In a year or two it will be like a second home to me for sure.

Studio was located near the entrance to the building on the base level. Mandy opened the door, the one you would expect from the gymnasium at your local school, and turned on the lights. We were at the top of the huge studio, thirty or more rows on both sides with stairs coming down to the main stage which was amazingly simple yet sophisticated. On the back, there was a Hollywood-end hill with the sign. It was not a picture more like a sculpture, 3D painting. Whatever it was, it looked very real to me. From both sides of the Hollywood-end sign, two sets of stairs were coming down to the main stage that was made of what? You guessed it right, one huge sofa and two beautiful desks on both sides. I looked at an interrogation setup but with all of the surrounding you had to be an idiot to think of it in this way. This made me even more eager to start this show as soon as possible. Maybe it brought some memories. I felt the same way before I got my own show in the past life. Believe me, it's something not so easy to forget. The thrill of having the ability to create everything from the scratch and seeing it grow is amazing. When people are enjoying it as much as you did creating, it is hard to describe. You have to live it to believe it.

- I love it Mandy. It looks wonderful, just wonderful.
- I like it too. They really did a great job with everything. And you were afraid that nothing is taken

care of. See all done.

- Oh Mandy. Done, but not by us. It's great that we both like it, but the true hosts should pay more attention to everything going around the show. We were just lucky.

- OK, OK, queen of talk shows. We will from now on, happy?
- You bet I am.

After the tour, we headed to give back the dresses and put our clothes back on our asses. Then a short detour to our boss. I felt regret that we gave back these gorgeous gowns. For sure, our entrance to the office would be more "flashy" and with a statement that we will rule next season.

I thought that Mary was my boss here at the station, but the real person in command of the TV shows was Timothy. From the first time I saw him I felt friendly vibes. I know that the feeling when you see someone at first sight is not always accurate and true. In his case, he must have been a really good actor to cover everything. He was really sincere.

- Ladies, so good to finally see you both in one room. Mandy, you look beautiful as always. Joan so very nice to meet you, I am Timothy. We had high hopes for the show for a long time. I am really pleased that you came at the time we needed most.

- Oh, thank you so much. I am very happy to be here.

☼ ☼ ☼

OK. I lied, sort of. I'd rather be alive and kicking in the world I left so suddenly. But knowing I have no other choice I suppose I am happy to be here too.

- I have seen the photos. I do not know which one of you had an idea with this one, but I love it and we're going to use it in the nationwide campaign for the show. Well done!

- We're glad you like it. We had a lot of fun during the shoot and the dresses were amazing. I sincerely hope that we will have such fabulous wardrobe for each episode of the show.

- You betcha. If you bring higher ratings for the network, you can have whatever you want.

- Mhmm, I will remember that.
- Do you have plans for first episode? Who are you going to invite. I am really curious.
- We are thinking about the whole Farthashians family. They will have season finale of their show, so we thought having them as our first guest would be a win-win situation. Don't you think?
- Superb thinking. Looking forward to the premiere. I have a meeting set for now, so I gotta run. It was a pleasure to see you both.

All the action in the studios really gave me a positive boost of energy before our big premiere show. We still have some work to do, how to play everything right. But we still have few days left to do so.

After an eventful day, this time I asked Mandy to go with me for a dinner. I did some research before we left for the vacation and found really nice sushi restaurant near the beach. We did not have much of a chance to enjoy the "rocky beaches" of Croatia, but today I must have a long walk on the sandy beach and eat something delicious afterwards.

CHAPTER TWENTY-SEVEN
Big premiere

For the remaining few days Mandy and myself were rehearsing the questions and planning everything. This is it. A big day for us and the all Hollywood-end citizens finally arrived. Today one of the biggest enemies of the true talent and grace will sink low. Every day teaches me more and more, even though I have been living for a long time now. This is my second life I know of. Our show was scheduled to be aired at 2 p.m.. Early in the morning, I was joined by Monique, Mandy, Ksav, and of course Mary. We all sat down for breakfast and were really happy with the upcoming show. Max was wandering around, probably thinking about his love left thousands kilometers away. We all had something against our guests, Ksav was used and mistreated by them every time she went to clean for them, Monique was almost brainwashed, and I never liked the rotten and conniving people. They don't even expect what will hit them right when it hurts most, the wallet of course. They are so plain; I don't even think they have any feelings left, as they already poorly acted them on the show.

The day was bright and sunny with little clouds here and there. This gave us even more positive energy to finish it right as we wanted. You see God, you wanted, you got it. First assignment is almost complete. We packed all necessary things and left for the studio few hours before the show. Yes, Max went with us too, why not it's our show so we can have whoever we want.

When we arrived, people were already waiting to be let in to the studio. The queue was long and it was really a good sign. There was a special section dedicated to special needs guests who might arrive on wheelchairs or require special treatment. I wanted it to be a friendly place to meet. I remember the talk shows from the past life where the audience was only treated as an accessory to fame and fortune of the hosts. This one will be different, everything will be different. I was not the only one who thought of it that way. Mandy was also very open for that type of improvements. She was even happy about it because she loves people and interaction with them. Of course down the road everything may change, we could have even more freaky guests and the audience may be not so approachable. I do not know. It is something I am willing to wait for. For the time being I want to enjoy our first victory with the most annoying family that ever graced the face of the Hollywood-end.

I was so happy to see all our guests that I decided to greet them in the queue. They were very excited and surprised by my gesture. They came here to spend some time with us, so why on earth I wouldn't spend some extra time with them. I am here for them. One thing crossed my mind and it was not something good. What if all those people are fans of Farthashians? If so, we are all so screwed. But I sincerely hope they are people who think and are interested to see some "quality" conversations and "undercover" footage.

Once we finished our "greet-meet" with audience awaiting the show, we entered the building. Max was so happy to finally have some sort of "red carpet" experience.

Our changing rooms were prepared. Guess what. I arranged a job for Kenny. He has been so marvelous with Monique; so we decided to have him around to take care of us for a change. The dresses for the premiere were exquisite. Mandy's orange gown was a masterpiece. She had her favorite wig on with gorgeous curls; so both of them gave a total package. My brown dress was not too bad either. It was finished with the faux fur collar. OK, I decided to quit wearing fur. Now I know it was an inappropriate thing to do. For sure, Max's reaction put me on the right path to quit it. We both looked glamorous.

All of the sudden, we got the information from the crew that the Farthashians family along with the managers (of course) arrived at the studio. Our adrenaline level jumped. Even though we had so many things up our sleeves, we couldn't be 100% sure how the show would come through. I asked Mandy to go and greet them. She was the only person they have never met. It would be risky to go there myself. Despite the fact that they have met me for a few minutes I could be recognized and then they could leave us with no guest on our premiere show we were eagerly waiting for.

Mandy returned from the meeting with a huge smile.

- Joan, OMG! The whole family arrived—Sin, her sisters, her mother, and her husband. I think we should ask for the body search. If they have guns, we might be in trouble, hahaha.

- I don't think they are so stupid to have anything "dangerous" for the show. I think they treat it as another publicity stunt, nothing else. Be right back honey. I have to go to a bathroom for a sec.

For a moment I thought, where the hell is Max? He is supposed to be keeping us company for the whole time. I went to the corridor and noticed Loey Farthashian leaning down to him. SHIIIITTT... I moved a bit closer.

- Hey little buddy. Do I know you? You look kind of familiar.

OK, now we would only need him to answer her "Yes babe we have met few days ago." But nothing like that happened. Max noticed me and started to walk in my direction.

- Seriously Max, don't you think she might recognize you?
- Do you really believe they have such good memory, I doubt it.
- Come on we're about to start.

The show was about to start. Mandy and I took our places behind the desks. An extra sofa was added to accommodate the whole Farthashians family without any problems. Audience was very eager for the show to start. They were applauding many times. All the cameras were ready and the huge screen was lowered down behind us. They made a brief test and started to run our intro which was fucking awesome. The music was contagious and the dynamics of the graphics plus our appearances were delivered the best way possible. I was really happy with the results. We even had an announcer.

Good Afternoon Hollywood-end! or should I say How you doin'. Prepare your next hour to be dazzled with great interviews, surprises, and fantastic guests. This is "How you doin' with Joan and Mandy."

OK, we could definitely improve this one. But it's not the most important thing right now. The clock was ticking and with a minute remaining to go live I got stressed. How is this even possible? Well it sort of was possible. I could do the stand-up and make people laugh to their last breath, but still it was kind of different experience from the one I had in the past and I couldn't possibly do it.

There was it. It started—lights, camera, and action. Our show intro video started to be displayed behind our backs, music started to play, and announcer started to talk about the show and today's guests. Audience was clapping and was very enthusiastic about the things that were about to be unfolded. Finally the lights focused on us and I started the show.

- I am so thrilled to see such a wonderful audience. You are flawless. Some of you I have already met in the queue. To the rest of you, a big Hello. Welcome to the premiere airing of the new show that focuses on Hollywood-end and its famous residents. We are now live on air on the biggest TV station in LA area, PTS. My name is Joan and I am a half of the team responsible for this TV show. Please meet my co-host and best friend Mandy Williamson.

- Thank you Joan. We are so happy to be here with you and for you. Today we have the guests from out of this world, literally, out of this world, one and the only Farthashians family.

People started to clap so loud I could barely recognize any voice coming from Mandy. When the Farthashians "graced" the stage, audience stood up and started to act like infatuated with them. Really, it didn't look good, at least from our perspective. Hopefully they will change their minds about them when they see what we have prepared for them.

We started easy with the questions about the continuous fame and fortune. After few minutes, I noticed strange grimaces on Loey's face. I think she started to remember the day I came for Max. Sin was really expressionless on her face. She barely was talking with us about anything private beside the show. Have Pamela managed to improve the procedure to be permanent? It's hard to tell. To check it out further we started to ask questions about Sin's seizures and that the people noticed her sudden changes of behavior. Of course, Pamela started to explain it with health problems and stressful situations. When our questions began to be more personal, Lamey started to act aggressively. His comments were disrespectful and with the tone I could not possibly approve.

Then we went to get the big guns. Mandy explained the audience that we're very worried about the well-being of the famous Farthashian and we think something should be done. As we worked on the footage to be only related to the freakish Sin's behavior, one short clip was showed. This made Lamey furious to the maximum. We didn't even start yet with the best stuff. Lamey stood up and started to act like a monkey on drugs (not that I know how it looks like, sorry it just came to my mind). Then it happened. Sin got her seizure, fell down to the floor, and started to scream. Lamey could not handle it. He took the bottle of water that was standing in front of them and threw it in our direction. Shit, we're not Jerry asshole. Bottle hit the screen behind our backs and we got a short circuit.

Everything got black, and people in the audience started to scream. Now that was something we could not predict. When the lights came back after a minute, few of our guests were missing. Pamela and Jacob disappeared ....

To be continued ....

Fun Facts

1. Rabac—this city actually exists in Croatia and most of the descriptions in this book are true. Only one thing is false: Rabac does not have an airport.

2. "Not So Terrible Advice" —actually *Terrible Advice* was performed several times in the autumn of 2011 at London's Menier Chocolate Factory Theatre. I had a privilege of attending one of the shows. Yes, we had first row seats and the description is 100% true. You should regret not being there. Show was amazing and I had an opportunity to meet Scott Bakula in person.

3. You might have noticed number "13" many times in the book. This is my favorite number and I lived at no. 13 all my life. Thirteen is following me anywhere I move.

4. Ksav—this character was based on my beloved Grandmother Ksawera, who passed away in 1996. She was an amazing woman who did so many things in life to support her family and keep everything rolling in the right direction.

Interact with the Author

Official website: www.rafalkudlinski.com

Visit Rafal's official profiles at :
Goodreads : www.goodreads.com/rafciok
Twitter: www.twitter.com/djelliott1002
Facebook: www.facebook.com/jrdropdeaddiva

Joan and the gang will return in : "How you doin' with Joan and Mandy"

notes

notes

notes

notes

notes

notes

www.ingramcontent.com/pod-product-compliance
Lightning Source LLC
Chambersburg PA
CBHW061431040426
42450CB00007B/990